The Rape of Innocence
Taking Captivity Captive

Lacresha N. Hayes

Foreword by Pastor Lensey C. Hayes

Living Waters Publishing Company
West Monroe, Louisiana

The Rape of Innocence: Taking Captivity Captive
Lacresha N. Hayes

Edited by: Kenna Simpson

Cover Art by: Susan Jagosz, California
Cover Layout by: Jason Grisham, Louisiana

ISBN 978-0-9798154-0-9

LCCN 2007906745

Christian inspirational

Published by Living Waters Publishing Company
www.livingwaterspc.com

Printed in the United States of America

Other Books by Author

Becoming: My Personal Memoirs
(formerly Whispers of the Heart)

Christian Principles series:
My Thoughts Exactly
Walk with Me
Book of Promises
All or Nothing
Heavenly Voices

Coming Soon!

Full Exposure

Justified

Introducing the Culpeppers

A Culpepper Easter

Dedications and Acknowledgments

To my mother, Dorothy: I thank God that we were able to begin our healing process together through my last book. Perhaps this book will complete our healing process and move us into the next dimension together. I love you for doing what you knew was best.

I would like to acknowledge the love of my life, my husband who sees me in the light of God's truth. Lensey, I truly appreciate you for fostering healing, growth, love and peace in my life. God uses you in my life, and in the lives of the multitude.

Foreword

Have you ever read a book that stayed with you long after you put it down, a book that moved you to tears, sometimes of joy, and sometimes pain?

As I watched my wife begin to write the most intimate details of her life and saw the tears shed over each page, I realized that this was a God-thing. No one exposes themselves to this degree except God moves upon them. In a time when privacy is golden, my wife has chosen to expose herself and her family for the healing benefit of multitudes. She wrote this book for you because chances are, if you are reading this book, you have, or someone close to you has, experienced some of the same things that she has.

Each page of this book leaves an impression of God's unfailing mercy, grace and love. I believe every reader will realize as they read that God is not a respecter of persons. What He did for Lacresha, He can and will do for you. My wife hasn't always been an author, business owner, student and minister. Once upon a time, not so long ago, she was a victim with a victim's mentality. She was lonely and lost. Yet, through the power of God, she gained victory. Abba God did a complete work in her life, just as He will in yours. When He delivers and heals, He brings complete deliverance and healing. He *will* do that for you.

Be encouraged. Realize that you can't judge the love of God according to your hardships. God's love transcends hardships. Neither can you judge His love by your blessings. The Bible says God rains upon the just as well as the unjust. His love is bigger than

4

blessings. Sometimes, to show the magnitude of passionate love He has for us, God has to subject us to torrential rains and storm clouds that weigh heavily upon us. Sometimes, to show us who we are in Him, He has to say "no" to the things we desire most. God's love cannot be measured by the happenings in our lives. It can only be measured by the great sacrifice that was made for our benefit when Jesus gave up His perfect life to save our imperfect lives. It can only be judged by the ultimate victory you will see if you hold on to Him!

Pastor Lensey Hayes
Compassionate Healing Ministries International

Introduction

Looking back, I was a relatively happy young child. I didn't have much of a sense of humor, but I knew how to have fun. I was a tomboy. I climbed trees. I chased bees and lightning bugs with mason jars. I swung on anything that would support my weight. I played softball and football, and I loved cap guns. They made a unique smell that I liked when I shot them.

Though I had my painful moments, how could I have known back then about all the horrible decisions I would make later? How could I have known about the many men that would parade through my life? How could I have known that the perversion in my family would nearly destroy me? It was learned behavior repeating itself!

People say that hindsight is 20/20. I sometimes still have mixed feelings about my past. I see so many things that I would have done differently. A part of me grieves the childhood that was sacrificed for the selfish and hurtful desires of the adults around me. That same part of me hurts for the little girl that made too many grown up decisions, decisions that would haunt her into adulthood and rob her of the joys of becoming. However, another part of me appreciates the pain. All of it worked together for my good, just like Romans 8:28 said it would. My experiences have helped me become a vessel that God can use.

This is not an easy story to read. It was not an easy story to live through, nor to write and share with the world. Still, if my pain can help someone else through theirs, then Amen and so be it. Many tears stain these pages: the tears of what I know, and of what I will never know, tears of pain and tears of joy!

Because of the things that happened to me, I often wonder at what age I'd have given up my virginity if it had not been stolen from me. I wonder at what age I would have decided to start a family. All of that remains a mystery to me. These are some of the milestones wherein the power to choose was stolen from me. For some of you who are reading this book, it was also stolen from you.

This is my story. It might be yours also. Unfortunately, it is a story that too many people can relate to. It is a story, repeated through history, which has destroyed lives and families. Nevertheless, it isn't all bad. This is *also* a story of victory and of the overcoming power of Jesus Christ. God made promises to me concerning this testimony. In obedience, I lay my life before everyone who will read this book. You are part of my promise from God. Because of you, I am able to tell what will probably sound like a tall tale to those who have never walked through it themselves. Yet, for those of us who have lived these pages, we know that there is yet even more to tell.

I pray that everyone reading this book finds healing and deliverance. I pray each reader finds strength in the truth. I pray that you will find a new intimacy with our Father. Use His strength to reclaim your life. Take it back and boldly proclaim, "There will be no more victims here." God's will be done with this book. Amen!

Please take advantage of the resources in the back of this book.

The Rape of Innocence

~Chapter 1~
Do The Shuffle... With My Life

My grandmother, until her death, was the center of my life. She had faults, but she always tried to take good care of me. No matter how much alcohol she drank, I never went hungry or naked, though I couldn't wear name brands. I couldn't participate in a lot of extracurricular activities at school. I didn't have the expensive toys. However, I did have a grandmother who tried to spoil me in her own way and to the best of her ability.

Even though my grandmother was illiterate, she was very proud. From the way she carried herself to the way her bills were always paid, an onlooker would never know she could barely sign her name. She was a beautiful older woman, her Indian heritage plain to see. She had long, silky gray hair that was gray when she was born. Her skin was rough, partly due to smoking and partly to an explosion that I was responsible for as a toddler. (I accidentally left the gas stove on, and when she went to light it, it blew up in her face... I vaguely remember it... I was very young.) She was spunky, and usually quite adorable. I lived with her for the majority of my childhood.

When we were in a pinch, my grandmother's uncle was often the one to bail us out. He was a feisty old man who carried a gun everywhere he went. Though he was in a wheelchair, he was very independent and took good care of himself and his blind wife. She could walk, but could not see. He could see, but could not walk. Is that not proof that God knows what we need, and that His mercy works for both the just and unjust?

I spent much of my time at their house when I was a child. I usually helped them by washing dishes, doing general cleaning and walking to the store. Sometimes, I would finish my homework at their house. He would always give me money for helping, or for the good grades that I regularly earned. Sometimes, I would have more money in my pockets than my grandmother. My great, great uncle "loved" me... and in all the wrong ways. I can't remember when it started, but I know how it ended.

Molestation, that Ugly Word

One day, my cousin and I went to clean my great, great uncle's kitchen and bathroom. After awhile, he sent her into the bathroom to clean. I was on my knees on his counter trying to clean the upper cabinets in the kitchen when he put his hand between my legs. I was eleven years old. By this time, though "it" was still uncomfortable, "it" had been going on for at least 4 years. I had gotten used to "it". He often gave me extra money when he touched me. It is frightening how easily a small child can learn prostitution!

After two or three minutes, my cousin came in and saw my uncle's hand between my legs. As we were leaving, I begged her not to tell anyone. She advised me she was going to tell her mother and that I should tell my grandmother. She was older than me and I usually listened to her, but this time was different. I had already been down that road. It had been so long that I had almost forgotten when I'd attempted to tell the first time. My grandmother had told me that I was probably misunderstanding him. She said he was just "friendly" like that. It didn't

10

appear that she cared, but appearances can be deceiving. Either way, I wasn't willing to trust anyone with my secret again.

In retrospect, I now realize that my grandmother had also been a victim of sexual abuse. She had experienced the shame, defenselessness, and vulnerability of having a trusted family member or friend of the family cross boundaries that shouldn't have been crossed. She, too, had felt abandoned. She had felt the rejection, the feelings of failure, and hopelessness that come with having your most prized possession stolen from you. I can imagine the first time I told her that her uncle was touching me; her thoughts were probably first denial, then hopelessness. After all, he helped us with bills, loaned us money and had been more of a father to her than his brother had. She couldn't defend herself; how could she defend me? She probably battled for years as I went through molestation.

Looking back, I believe my grandmother tried the only thing she could think of to offer me some protection. In her mind, she felt she couldn't ask him out of our lives, but she could give me advice. Every time she sent me over there, she would always say, "Hurry back," or "Be careful and come right back."

My cousin remained true to her word. She told her mother that night and her mother came to tell my grandmother the next morning. My grandmother was outraged! I suppose the truth had been exposed in a way that disarmed her and ended the denial that had protected her from having to take action for years.

11

My grandmother confronted her uncle, however difficult it was. Of course, he denied it with all sorts of profanity aimed at both my grandmother and myself. Though I was not the one to spill the beans, I was the "liar;" I was the "troublemaker". Never mind that someone *else* had seen him do it. Even *that* was "my fault" because I couldn't explain what an old man's hands were doing between my thighs in the first place. I was bewildered! I was hurt! I was ashamed! I was downright furious... I couldn't decide which emotion was right. I decided to feel nothing - I let numbness come.

Shuffling

I was eleven years old when my mother came to pick me up from Warren, Arkansas. Somehow, she'd found out about the situation. Looking back, my mother never doubted for one second the truth surrounding these incidents. I suppose issues in her own past had a lot to do with her quick belief and reaction to this new information.

My mother is something of a spirited woman. She is a true fighter. She was always quick to speak her mind, and even quicker to throw the first punch. Growing up hard had a lot to do with that. In a rage, not only for me but for herself also, she drew the line. She decided she would raise me herself from that point on.

Some part of me was very happy because I loved my mother and had always wanted to be with her. However, I loved my grandmother just as much. I didn't want to leave her; she was everything to me! She had raised me and she was my stable foundation. My grandmother was my "mother" too... she was "mama," and she had been for a long time. How was I to make it without her? I didn't have a clue. I knew for sure that my mother would be a lot tougher on me. I knew that she wouldn't probably spoil me like "mama" did. Things would change, I knew for sure. And as much trepidation as that built up in me, it didn't kill the excitement at a chance to be with my mother. So, I made my home in the capital city of Arkansas, a larger, faster-paced city that only afforded more opportunities for me to be taken advantage of.

If problems could be solved by moving, what a happy world this would be. Unfortunately, when we run from one problem, we usually run into another one, two, three or four.

~Chapter 2~
The Move

I loved my mother's second husband. They married when I was three or four years old. He was very handsome and charming. He looked a lot like the R & B singer, Maxwell. He was tall and strong. I felt safe with him for a very long time.

When I was young, I thought he was the most handsome dad a girl could ask for. I even preferred him over my grandmother's boyfriend who had been with my grandmother since my mother was a young child. I called him daddy too, but my mother's husband was by far the one I trusted and believed in. He treated me the way I thought a dad should treat his daughter.

My stepfather often spoiled me. I never doubted that he loved me. I never felt like I was a stepchild with him. It was as if I were his biological daughter. To some degree and at various times, I think I might have placed him on a pedestal. He was precious to me because he helped to ease the pain of a biological father that was absent from my life.

My stepfather and my mother went through many tough situations, many trials and storms. They even determined to make their marriage survive extreme domestic abuse. He shot her twice, once through the arm and into her side, and once in the back. She was hospitalized for a very long time behind that incident. Even now, she still has a bullet lodged inside her from that incident. Later on, she stabbed him, opening his stomach so wide that he had to hold his intestines in with his hand as he ran for help. Obviously, they had no fairy tale marriage by a long shot. He beat her with a pine log on another occasion and she put a permanent dent in his forehead with the heel of her shoe. I grew up watching and hearing about this kind of violence all my life. It damaged me severely, but at that time, I didn't know it.

Even through all the things that my stepfather did to my mother - from beating her to almost overdosing her with drugs when she did not take drugs - I never hated him. I loved him in spite of it all. I loved her too. I never wanted to come to the crossroads where I would have to choose between the two of them, but unfortunately, that day eventually did arrive. I always believed they could fix things. I was very young and very simple in my thinking. I never wanted them to split up because I thought they were meant to be together. Though many times my good thoughts toward him were tested, in the end, he was always still my "daddy" and I was still his daughter.

I do not want to tell my mother's story. Maybe one day she will tell her own. Until that time, suffice it to say, her testimony is much more alarming than mine is. Still, our lives ran much the same harrowing course for a long season. I went through some very difficult things because of her. Mom tried her best to spare me from them, but it was not in her power to do so. In her efforts to protect me, things sometimes got worse.

My stepfather's family was very large. I think he had two sisters and four brothers. Both of his sisters had many children. One of them in particular always stood out to me. His name was Mark. He was much older than I was, but to me, he was the "living

15

end!" I was *so* infatuated! I just *knew* that he was my boyfriend, never minding the fact that he was my step cousin and a full grown, albeit young man. He knew I had a major crush on him, but for the most part, he dealt with me very little... at least at first. Little did he know I had much more experience than any other eleven year old he had ever known. My body had been coming alive slowly over the years due to the molestation that I had already endured. This man was subject of my second crush (the first being when I was in kindergarten, when I'd liked a little white boy named Jason), my step cousin Mark was eight and a half years older than me, and he was about to change my life. My life would not be changed because of him directly, but indirectly, dangerously, the crush I had on him would take me down a terrible path for a pre-teen to travel.

My body began to fill out at a very young age. I was shapely even as a baby and people in the neighborhood would always say that I was going to be a heartbreaker. They failed to mention the number of times my own heart would break. Almost everyone who met me thought I had a beautiful shape. People were always commenting on my bowed legs, or my hips or my thighs. I got "pretty" comments too, but most of the comments were about my body. Near the age of ten, I began to take on the form of a woman in some ways. Full breasts were the only things I lacked. By the time sixth grade started in Little Rock, Arkansas, I was shaped like a fifteen or sixteen year old. I had also willfully engaged in sexual activities by this time, primarily because of my early exposure to the sexual world.

I was always intelligent. I never had to study because I soaked up knowledge like a sponge. I loved school and I loved to learn. I also loved to learn from people. I picked up many bad habits. I never considered myself dumb, but in ignorance, I played that role to perfection for a long season in my life. I had begun to have sex willingly because I was tired of people taking it from me. I felt that the easier thing to do would be to give it away. Certainly, I figured it would hurt less and maybe even afford me certain safety benefits. I began to think of myself as an adult and tried to behave as one, yet I still possessed a child's mind. Much heartbreak followed closely behind my faulty reasoning.

~Chapter 3~
An Outhouse and Well Water

I remember the summer I moved to Little Rock. I loved it there at first, but I missed my grandmother like crazy. Still, I loved being with my stepfather and my mother. Sometimes, they were a barrel of laughs. Sometimes, I almost forgot about the trauma I had already experienced. There were times when we almost felt like a real family. "Almost" being the operative word here.

One day, soon after my arrival in the big city, we all decided to walk down to a friend's house. Nukie was a great friend of the family. She had dated my grandfather a long time before, but her and my mom stayed friends for life. They were about the same age... my grandfather was known for that kind of stuff. I loved going to Nukie's because her daughter, Sharon, and I were best friends. I actually considered Sharon to be my sister. She was two years older than me and I loved being around her.

After visiting awhile, we began our trek back home in the sweltering summer heat. While walking home, mopeds began to circle us. Three teenage boys on two mopeds continued to circle us and finally followed us home. I had just arrived in Little Rock that previous weekend and this was a Tuesday. I will never forget it.

After we got home, the tallest of the teens, Junior, came and knocked on the door of our little one room house. My stepfather and my mother thought it was funny that he actually had some manners. My mother knew Junior's dad and so agreed to allow him to call me. It was so awesome to me that he was four or five years older than me, yet still liked me. In my mind, he was my "Mr. Tall, Dark and Handsome". I still had a crush on Mark, but I kind of *knew* that Mark was just a childish crush... Junior seemed more like the real thing! He was at least 6'2 even then. He had a smooth caramel complexion and an awkward voice that hadn't completed its change yet.

Junior was my first "real" boyfriend and my first willful experience with sex. We talked on the phone every night. We stayed in trouble because we would fall asleep on the phone with each other. We played music for each other. We had what seemed to me a real courtship. It was wonderful, and for a little while I felt carefree again, like the child that I was. Moreover, since he lived across the street from Sharon, I saw him each time I spent the night at her house. We played and we chased each other and I had fun. I can still remember that woeful night things changed as if it were just yesterday.

Sharon taught me the art of "mooning" people. I did not particularly like it, but I did it because she did. We mooned the boys all night one night. They mooned us back. That was such a ridiculous game to play, but it made me feel free from adult worries. The next morning, we stayed home most of the day and played with Junior and his twin cousins. Sharon was dating one of the twins; I was dating Junior, and everything seemed perfect. At that young age, I really thought that we would grow up and marry those boys.

Later on that second night, Sharon talked to me about "giving up my virginity". To her, even if someone had taken my virginity, if I had not given it

19

up, then I was still a virgin. She gave me one of her birth control pills. I was so nervous! In fact, I was nearly scared to death! My heart skipped beats, then beat too much, erratically jumping in my chest! I was sweating while my body shook with anxious chills all at the same time. I had no idea what to do! I was only eleven years old and had no clue how to respond to a boy that I actually liked, but I had decided to "go all the way". Going "all the way" proved to be painful and embarrassing. It was a very emotional moment for me. I cried - hard. The tears just would *not* stop rolling down my face! I sobbed because my nether-regions throbbed with pain, even though he'd tried to be gentle - it had been sheer torture! My young body was not prepared for him, and I tore excruciatingly. I also cried naive tears because I thought I was in love with him; I even told him so. He tried to comfort me some, and shortly thereafter he left to go home while I continued to cry and tried to stop myself from bleeding.

The next day, the fantasy of being in love came crashing down all around me. Junior made fun of me all day long. He told all his friends that I was a virgin and I was laughed to scorn. That hurt me so badly! He kept chanting and laughing, saying that I wasn't a woman. I hadn't actually been a virgin, except in my own mind, and in his; and surely I was most definitely *not* a woman! I was an eleven-year-old child. I couldn't take their jeering so I went home.

Our home sported an outhouse and a well instead of running water. A part of me wanted to jump into the well and see if anyone would truly miss me, but instead I went into the foul, dark outhouse and sat there hopelessly swatting at flies, sweating, and trying to stem the flow of tears. I felt so rejected and humiliated! I felt like a tramp, or a slut, or something awful like the words I'd heard people use to refer to me so many times before; then, just when I thought things could not get any worse, they did!

~Chapter 4~
What Now?

My mother and stepfather lived in a one-room house so I slept in a bed with them. My mother slept in the middle and I slept on the side nearest the front door. One early morning, she sent me next door to my grandfather's house. I don't remember what caused me to turn around and go back home, but I did. As I got close to the house, I heard them arguing. My mother was accusing my "daddy" of fondling me while I was asleep. He said that he thought he'd been touching her. At first, she wasn't buying it, but she finally conceded, knowing that she could not prove he was lying. But something in the back of my own mind told me that he was lying indeed. I had a memory that disturbed me, though it was not very clear, and I felt as if it could have been a dream.

I remembered how I used to pretend I was asleep so that I could get back on the phone with Junior. On one of those nights, it seemed as if I could remember him reaching around my mom and touching me while looking down at me from the other side of her. Was that a dream or did it really happen? Because I was not absolutely positive, I never mentioned it.

When they finished arguing, she'd decided to send me to stay with my grandfather. He only lived across the yard, but I wanted to stay with my mother. It seemed her decision always haunted me because I knew deep down that she should have done something else. I felt as if she should have left and stayed next door with me. She stayed at home with her husband. I went next door to my grandfather's house alone.

22

No Safe Place

From time to time, different people would spend the night with my grandfather. He had a somewhat open door policy. One of my stepfather's nieces had a boyfriend. Sometimes when they argued, he would come and stay at my grandfather's house. He was a very grown man, somewhere around my mother's age. He came to stay the night one time while I was living with my grandfather. It was very late and I was asleep. My grandfather and his girlfriend were in the other room asleep. Everyone had partied late into the night, but I had gone to bed in the middle of all the excitement.

At some point, in the wee morning hours, I remember waking up because I felt a weird sensation between my legs. This man had his mouth between my legs. I told him to stop and leave me alone or I would tell. He told me I would get in trouble. He threatened me in a very roundabout manner and said some very harsh things. Then he tried to convince me that what he was doing was normal and it wasn't wrong. By that time, I felt that even if I did tell it, nothing would happen. I felt as if I had no choice.

I zoned out, stared blankly at the ceiling, and let him have his way with me. His way turned out to be "all the way". It hurt, but I just wanted it to end as soon as possible so I didn't struggle. I cried silently, but on the inside I began to harden. The next morning, he threatened me again and told me to "walk right" and then he left. I went to the steamy, nasty outhouse and glad for the privacy, I cried some more. I felt abandoned and unloved. I hated that man and I hated myself. I hated my mother, my uncle, my

23

stepfather, and all of the drunks in my life. But of them all, I think I placed most of the blame on my mother. I blamed her for coming to get me from my grandmother. I blamed her for not being at my grandfather's with me. I was still eleven years old and my eyes were opening to sex in the worst way possible. I began to hate how I looked. I hated my body and I hated the person who gave it to me… in my own mind, it was even my mother's fault that I had her shape. I was becoming angrier by the day. My heart was growing cold, and I was still only a child. I felt that my becoming hard was my only defense system. For a very long time, it was. But, like all stays that are not of God, it failed me. Of course, it was by God's hand that it was removed, and His timing is perfect. Still, to me, it felt like His timing couldn't have been worse.

It would be easy to fill this chapter with story after traumatic story, because in my young life, there was always one thing after another. It seems before one pain would subside, another would come and take over. Before one humiliation was out of my mind, another would join forces with it to torment me all the more, day after day, and night after agonizing night.

An eleven-year-old child shouldn't have hundreds of regrets and legions of fears. At that age, regrets should center on wearing the wrong shoes or accidentally breaking a dish or toy. Fears should be centered on getting an occasional spanking for arriving home from playing later than expected, or being hit by a car if careful attention is not paid when crossing the street. Eleven year old girls fear bugs, snakes and sometimes the dark. Unfortunately, that was not the way of my life or the nature of my fears.

I had more regrets at eleven than many people will ever have. I had to grow up very fast. In my mind, *someone* had to do something to protect me. There had to be a safe place for me *somewhere*. Those dark thoughts nagged at me until they consumed me. I think that if I had ever actually found that safety somewhere, I would never have returned from it.

~Chapter 5~
Granite Mountain of Peace...
for a Moment

My stepfather had a sister who had six daughters and one son. Her baby girl, Moonie, was my age and we were very close. I loved going over to her house. We always had fun together, staying outside until all times of the night. There were many kids in the area in which she lived. We went swimming a lot. We rode bikes up and down the hill; we played basketball and kick-ball. I really loved being around my aunt, her husband and her kids.

My time there was always a reprieve for me, though I got in trouble a lot for stealing, a habit I had picked up from some other kids. If I was not in trouble for that, I got in trouble for fighting, or rather *not* fighting. I was not much of a fighter, but my aunt's youngest daughter and I fought all the time. I actually got *most* of my spankings for either not fighting back, or for losing a fight I should have won. They never understood why I hated the violence so much. Not surprisingly, my nerves were bad as a child and I had no tolerance for violence. The whole idea of inflicting pain upon someone else was sickening to me. But, just as my grandmother used to prophesy, the beast eventually *did* come out of me, to the dismay of many.

My aunt's son had a troubled history. He was often in trouble for burglary and the like. He had been in and out of jail quite a bit. I remember one early morning at my aunt's when the whole house was sleeping: I woke up to use the bathroom. As I was walking through the living room, he grabbed my arm and pulled me down to the floor. More annoyed than alarmed, I assumed he just wanted to play rough, or to wrestle as he usually did. All of us did that frequently there. I told him to stop because I was still sleepy and didn't feel like playing. I was tired because we had all stayed up late. He was not playing at all.

As he yanked me down to the floor, I realized he really wanted to have sex with me. I was terrified! Immediately, my head began to reel. I tried to fight him off, regretting the day I'd started biting my nails, but he had me before I knew it. It lasted all of two minutes. It happened so quickly that I wondered if it had happened at all. He made me go to the bathroom and clean myself up. I was torn some, and it hurt to wash myself. It was dreadful! I felt disrespected, but I dared not say anything to anybody. What would they do except blame me?

That was the first time I ever seriously considered suicide. At the ripe old age of eleven, I was devastated! In my mind, I had no adequate defenses and zero allies. Probably, there were some who'd have been on my side, but I knew of none. I did not know on that day that thoughts and attempts at suicide would play a great part in my life. Nevertheless, that was when the fight between survival and the twisted desire for death and blessed nothingness commenced. It was then that my battle became a life and death matter. It started there, the day when I no longer felt innocent. I felt guilty and ashamed of being myself. I began to blame myself and thought surely no one else in the whole world could be going through this kind of mess. What sort of child had this type of thing going on in their lives so frequently? To this day, I've not found anyone else who's been in that situation as many times as I was,

27

and with so many different people. I felt unloved then, and sometimes, even now, I struggle with that same feeling.

I don't think that most people realize the importance of their actions to another person's life. Callousness, selfishness and cruelty can destroy lives. Contrary to popular (and comfortable) opinion, our issues *do* affect others. What we do, say, and think has an impact on everything around us.

It was never my choice to feel unloved. It wasn't my choice to deal with suicidal thoughts. Before I was old enough to choose, I was already dealing with adult issues because of the actions of others. I grew up feeling so negative about myself that it took many progressive moves of God to bring me through it. I had years of practice in hating myself. It would take years of ministry for me to love myself again, and to realize that I deserved to be loved by others.

~Chapter 6~
Where Is the Love

The same gut-wrenching sensations I felt as a child come back to me as I put pen to paper about my life. I can still feel the pain and I am acutely aware of all the humiliation I endured as a child. Even so, reliving those memories has provided a more complete healing for me. It is a letting go and a necessary purge. As an adult, I can clearly see that much of what I blamed myself for then was truly not my fault. As a minister, I know that God had His hands in it all. Even in the deepest depths of despair, He was with me. He trusted me to endure what many others could not so that through my hardship, I may minister to others.

As sixth grade began, I took more notice of Mark, my crush. He was six feet tall and dark complexioned with full lips. He would engage in lively conversation with me and often called me his "little" girlfriend, but he kept saying I was too young to really be his girlfriend. One of his older brothers did not share that same conviction. One day, as I was in their bedroom, his brother walked in. I often went in the room when no one was home. I liked laying on his roomy bed and on their soft carpet, neither of which we had at home. Mark's brother shared a room with him, but he was rarely home. This particular morning though, he came in and began to talk to me. Until then, he had usually ignored me.

Mark's brother went into his duffle bag and pulled out a condom, which he passed to me. I had no idea what it was. I was still very green in many areas. He said that we would use it later. I asked him

29

what it was, but he just grinned without answering me. Even if he *had* told me, I still would not have understood what a condom was. I had never heard of a condom at that point. I kept playing with the package. It was a little small rectangle and it felt slippery and wet through the package. At first, it seemed like it could be lotion, but it had a hard ridge in there somewhere. I thought that maybe it was a water balloon and settled in my mind that indeed it was a balloon.

Later on, my mother came to walk me home. I walked out of the house with it in my hand. I told my mom that it was a water balloon. She asked me who gave it to me and I told her; I also told her what he'd said. She was furious! I'd always thought my mom had a bad temper, so to my thinking, she was just over-reacting again. She asked me if I had been touched. I said no. Then my mom told me to show it to my stepfather when I got home. When we arrived home, I ran into the house and told daddy what happened, showing him my "balloon" for his inspection and approval. He was just as angry as my mom had been and I was totally confused. He informed me that my balloon was actually a condom. I was still lost. My parents almost could not believe I did not know what a condom was. Daddy then explained to me the purpose of a condom and I was mortified.

My stepfather raced to his sister's house and started a big commotion. After all the fussing and complaining and near violence, and after all the dust had settled, guess who the blame rested with? If you guessed me, you hit the nail on the head. It was supposedly my fault for being in the room. It was my fault for being over there so much, and so forth and so on. My stepfather and my mother tried to defend me, but as for as everyone else, they blamed me. They accused me of being loose and flirtatious. They said I was the problem. They treated me as if I had no feelings or emotions. I was devastated by the cruelty of my in-laws' family so I stayed away for a long while. It was just another happenstance in a long line of them. I was never sure which of the incidents were actually my fault, neither was I sure which were not. I hardened myself a little bit more and pushed on. I was still a scant eleven years old.

I endured a lot at that age. In a time when I should have been playing hopscotch or jumping ropes, I was figuring out what a condom was and trying to avoid rape.

Late one summer night, my mother and I walked to the corner store to use the payphone. The store itself had closed much earlier, but the payphone was outside so we could still make calls after store hours. As we were standing there, two men in a small S-10 truck passed by. They circled back and stopped. They were trying to pick us up. Immediately, my mother, having lived in Little Rock for a long time, discerned that we were in danger. My mother whispered to me, telling me that when she said "go", we should run in two different ways. She seemed frightened, which in turn scared me. The truck was facing toward the direction we would have walked home so she ran that way. Faster than I thought was possible, I ran in the other direction. I was so afraid! I ran as fast and as far as I could until my legs were strained and my breath was gone. At that point, I dove between some bushes and a fence. The bushes provided some covering from the main street right there beside me, but the continuous barking of nearby dogs unnerved me just as much as if I had continued to run.

My mother happened to bump into one of my stepfather's nephews. The men in the truck then gave up on her and started looking for me. I heard them circling. I did not move a muscle, though my heart was beating in my throat and sweat was blurring my vision and coating my palms. My fear was amplified because I thought surely they would notice the dogs that were nearly on top of me, barking ferociously. They never did. All of a sudden, my mom's voice rang out in the dark. I also heard a man's voice calling me. I was scared to respond, but I did, hoping that she would hear me before the men did. My mom and her nephew had found me and saved me from certain rape and probable death. I knew then that Little Rock was not the place for me; and yes, I was still only eleven years old.

Many times over the course of the school year, I was either molested or raped. I had more narrow escapes than anyone I know. I suppose if I told it all, I would need to write two books. Suffice to say that I learned to separate my mind from my body just to keep my sanity. It seemed that the more men took liberties, the more I gave those liberties away so that it would not hurt as bad. But I hated… I hated deeply, and loathing overfilled my hardened heart. Hatred began to control me. I was depressed and pitiful, doing things then that as an adult I have had to be healed from. The things that were done to me, and the things I did, caused me to become a horrible person. I was trifling indeed, and I didn't care about anyone… not even myself. I took my cues from the people around me. They treated me as if I was nothing and nothing nice I became. I didn't have a reason to be nice. I didn't have a reason to care about others. In my mind, no one cared about me. I thought I was free. Little did I know I was bound in the deepest of pits, trapped by my own twisted mind-set.

The angry method of coping I chose probably hurt me worse than the actual rapes, countless molestations or my abandonment issues had. Because I was tired of fighting to keep my body to myself, I didn't value it anymore. Sex was not precious or exclusive. To me, it was a given- something a girl had to do, one way or the other.

I carried this attitude into both of my two failed marriages, and it was the reason lots of things didn't work out for me for a very long time.

~Chapter 7~
My Married Man

By the time I turned twelve, I had gone all the way with three people willingly and five unwillingly; I'd also been molested to various degrees throughout most of my young life. After school let out, I moved back to my small hometown of Warren, Arkansas. I was back in the place where it all began, but I was a very different person than the comparably innocent child that had left there only one year earlier. I fully understood that men loved sex. Most of them liked women who gave it up, though of course none of them *married* women like that. I had many preconceived ideas, and most of them were wrong.

Through trial and error and a string of quite a few men, one finally came along who cared for me. I know he probably was not the only one that did, but he was one of the few whom I believed when he said he loved me. Milton was married and had a son already. Of course, he did not volunteer that information when I met him. Even if he had, I am not sure that I would have cared at all. We began to see each other when I was twelve and he was twenty years old.

I met Milton through another friend. He seemed so sweet. He was gentle and patient with me, like a father. He was just tall enough for me to feel like he was tall, though in reality, he is average height for a man. He was dark complexioned with beautiful, sleepy eyes. I liked him immediately. He was eight years older than me. But, I lied and told him I was sixteen years old. I think he probably always knew I was younger than that, but he had no clue that I was as young as twelve years old. I had a beautiful shape

34

and I was mature for my age. I regularly skipped school to be with him, especially when he was not working. We began to spend a lot of time together.

Through a series of events, and to protect Milton from prosecution by the law, I ended up spending time in a home for delinquents. I stayed there for a little over a month. When I got out, my oldest brother talked to my grandmother and got her to let me "officially" see Milton. She reluctantly went for it. She wanted to do anything to keep me in school and off the streets. She made him agree to help her keep me in school, and so began my first relationship with a married man. Our relationship lasted seven years, throughout my entire childhood and into my college years.

By the time I was fourteen years old, I was pregnant by Milton. He had been buying my school clothes and taking me back and forth to school. My grandmother appreciated him for that. He had helped tame me quite a bit, but not totally. My grades never slipped, but I was still something of a wild child. I still had very little respect for myself or anyone else. My stony heart was numbed by pain, and it was going to take a process to help me begin to feel again.

When I was fifteen, Milton and I welcomed our son, Montario, into the world. He was a beautiful, healthy baby boy. I think a part of me melted when I saw him for the first time. My son helped me slow down a bit more, but ultimately, before he was born, my nature had become that of a person with few loyalties. I still was unsure of how to love. I knew I was supposed to love my son, and truly I did to the best of my ability. But, because of my lengthy, twisted past, I was scared, even of him. For years, I battled

35

with loving even my own child, partly because he was male and partly because I believed that love was the reason my heart hurt so much. A small amount of faithfulness came upon me the day I held my son for the first time, but it was more uncomfortable than peaceful.

Because of my many infidelities, mostly because of a learned behavior, and sometimes because I felt compelled to use sex to survive, Milton resorted to what he knew. He began to hit me. The physical abuse, in my mind, wasn't an issue for me. It never made me want to leave him. I suppose I'd learned to accept abuse as normal because I had grown up in an abusive home. He *said* he loved me, but he also wanted to hang on to his wife. He didn't trust me and I never blamed him for it since I didn't even consider myself trustworthy. I disrespected his wife in every way I could think of. Eventually, there came a time when they split up, but my relationship with Milton only got worse. I think he might have always blamed me for ruining his relationship with his wife.

I actually did love Milton as much as I could love a man. He had helped me to stay in school. He'd helped me to come back toward reality. Still, another part of me hated him, and I felt great animosity in my heart toward him because he'd slept with me. I guess it was like a double-barreled shotgun: I loved him for being there and for making me feel somewhat secure and safe. However, I began to perceive his actions toward me had been just as wrong as anyone else's actions toward me had been. To add insult to injury, in my own mind, I despised the fact that he would not marry me. I felt that after six years, he should have married me. In my perverse mind, I thought he surely owed me that much, didn't he? He was wiser than I gave him credit for though. He knew I was too young and too troubled to be married at that time.

I wanted to spite him. I wanted to get back at him… I married his nephew. I could have married anybody, but I chose to use Milton's nephew because I hated Milton for not giving in to me. Looking back, I was still very much that little lost girl who wanted to make everybody in my life prove his or her love for me. My thinking was warped. My heart was cold, and there seemed to be no hope for me anywhere.

When I married my first husband, I wasn't really thinking of *his* feelings. I just wanted to be married. I thought that would bring some completion to my life, as if it was an answer of sorts. He was my friend and I ruined our friendship by using him to get back at his uncle.

In all truth, though my relationship with someone eight years my senior and only ten years my mother's junior **was** a bad idea, it presented some boundaries and a degree of protection that quite possibly saved my life.

I've learned that nothing is wasted with God. Though I would never recommend statutory rape, which is exactly what he repeatedly engaged in, it was to my benefit in this case. My relationship with Milton most definitely kept me from much worse situations; he acted as protector, keeping me out of the streets, and he insisted I go to school. It all worked for my good.

37

~Chapter 8~
He Married an Axe Murderer

Here I was, nineteen, married and lonely. I only had thoughts of revenge to keep me warm. I wanted revenge on my family, on Milton, on his family, and even on myself. I was determined to go into the Air Force and fly fighter jets. I had been in so much trouble already though, that I didn't qualify to go. It seemed in so many ways, I had gotten married for nothing.

After getting married, a part of me began to soften a little bit more. I cared for my first husband. He had been one of my best friends before we got married. Honestly, I knew in my gut that I had taken advantage of Kinte. But, he was a gentle young man and quite patient with me. Kinte truly *did* love me to the best of his young ability, but he did not fully *know* me. He saw me through such innocent eyes that I began to love him back, to best of my undeveloped ability. He was so much fun to be with, and he was so naïve, that being with him helped me to forget who I really was at that time. We had a different kind of chemistry. It wasn't sexual… it was something more. When I was with him, it felt as if I were recapturing some lost part of my childhood. He was not like any man I had ever known. He was well-groomed, polite and helpful without thoughts of what he would get in return.

As I slowly began to let my guard down, I noticed many contrasts in my marriage. Still, I was determined to have a "normal" marriage regardless of why we got married in the first place. After we were married for a few months, my husband moved to Memphis, Tennessee for a job. When the holidays rolled around, he arranged for me to visit him in Memphis, and we spent Christmas and New Years together there. When the time came for me to return home, he had missed me so much that he decided to quit his job and return home with me. That was a major problem for me. It put a huge glitch in the comfortable lifestyle I had created for myself. You see, the whole while he was gone, I had enjoyed having my men friends help me pay bills and shop for whatever I thought I wanted. I was gratified in living that life. Now with him coming back home, things would be much more difficult.

Kinte was one of the first to tap into what little was left of my conscience. There was something about his trusting nature that made me feel bad when I did certain things. Even so, one day after we got back from Memphis, we got into an enormous fight! One of my guy friends had seen me walking to the video store and stopped in. Though I was not talking to him, my husband walked in and automatically assumed that something was going on. He practically dragged me out of the store. We fought all the way home. The fight wasn't that bad at first, but it was public, and I felt humiliated. Right there on the street, my husband hit me so hard that something snapped inside of me. It made me stop crying instantaneously. When we finally walked into our apartment, everything exploded. I stabbed and nearly killed him.

At the onset, he brandished two knives, giving me one of them. I don't know what he was thinking! I guess he supposed that I would have gotten one on my own had he not given it to me. It was a blessing that these were the cheaper brand of knives from the dollar store.

When Kinte laid his knife on the couch between us, I stared at it for what seemed to be an eternity. He continued to fuss at me. Then, I snapped! A blind rage came upon me! I already had one knife and I grabbed his. I tried to stick his through his left side; I jumped on top of him and began to stab at his face with mine. I didn't realize that one blade had popped out of its handle. Kinte pushed me off his lap and ran to the door. I chased him and he ended up trapped behind the door. On a rampage, I was still swinging both the knife and the handle of the one that I didn't realize was broken. The intact blade scratched his face and chest.

He finally reached out to push me a little further away. When he did, the blade went completely through his arm, severing ligaments, tendons and nerves. It also nearly severed a major vein. Blood spurted everywhere, from the ceiling to the floor.

He was only able to push me off because my grandfather walked in and distracted me. I could hear my son screaming from what seemed to be miles away. In reality, he was only a foot or two away. Kinte ran out the door with me on his heels. My cousin's girlfriend from next door helped save him. She grabbed me and tried to take the knife from me. Quickly, another girl joined in trying to wrest the knife from me. The second girl was almost killed when I swung the blade at her throat and missed by only a centimeter. Finally, my cousin's girlfriend was able to calm me down. She made me realize that my son was scared and sobbing hysterically. My husband then walked up to me and took his hand off his wound and said in an almost pitiful and incredulous voice, "Look what you did to me!" Blood was shooting out the top of the wound and pouring out

40

the bottom. It scared me so bad that I ran. I ran to my grandmother.

My grandmother and her boyfriend came out when they heard me screaming and saw me running. He was able to get the knives from me. It was then that I realized one of the blades was missing. He ran and hid the weapons while my grandmother tried to get me to stop screeching and calm down. She was petrified, thinking that I had killed someone. Blood was everywhere. I couldn't tell her anything because I had almost forgotten it all just that quickly. I only knew that my husband had been stabbed and he said that I did it. I couldn't believe that I was capable of something like that. When the memories did come back, the realization that I could do such a thing tormented me for years.

This was a horrible situation and I hated myself for it. I knew that it wasn't *our* fight that made me stab him, but the culmination of the build up of pain, anger and fear from over the years. It was all the men who had hit, raped and molested me. It was my own bad choices. It was the animosity I held toward my mother, my father and my grandmother. It was the convergence of every abominable thing that had ever happened to me, or that I had ever done, being taken out on my husband for a singular offense.

Kinte quickly forgave me for stabbing him. I went to be with him in the hospital. His family abhorred me, but he still loved me. I knew it was over between us though. I just did not want our marriage. I assisted him in every way I could until he recovered as much as possible. I pushed him to enroll in college and tutored him in certain subjects. But for me, the marriage was over. For a season, we remained close friends; he did not want to give me up. He had no clue why I was rejecting him. I knew that I wasn't right for him, and I certainly didn't want to damage him any further. I was on a guilt trip because he'd nearly lost his hand. He *still* can't use it like I can use mine. The doctor said it would never get better and I couldn't live with that, and especially not with watching it everyday.

Over the course of my life, I was beaten many times. I used to say if someone were to hit me, I would leave, yet it never seemed that simple. I had watched my mom and my grandmother go through physical and verbal abuse. I had watched them both be beaten to a bloody pulp, and I had even tried to protect them. Before I knew it, though, I was going through the same stuff. Worse yet, my son watched it all. After the out-of-control incident with my first husband, it took months before my son, Tario, stopped being afraid of me. I didn't want that lifestyle for my baby.

In all of the abusive relationships I have been in, I did what most women do. I ignored the bad and focused on the good. I reasoned inside myself that if I had not done something to provoke whichever one of them it was at the time, then they would have never hit me. Eventually, I would always find a way to place the blame on myself. Still, because abuse had been so prevalent in my family, I despised anyone that would put their hands on me. I became a vindictive, cold-hearted and violent woman who would go to any lengths for revenge. It wasn't right, but it was the only way I knew. In fact, I learned to appreciate the agony on a man's face when something was taken from him. It was through my first husband, though, that I learned that violence is never the answer. It would

take many years for me to forgive myself for hurting
him. It would also take many years to process the
violence out of my system.

Effects of Violence on Children

Violence was the norm in my life. I had gone
from being a peace-loving child who would not
defend myself, to actually stabbing people. I went
from being a victim to making others into the victims.
Even so, I could never shake the nagging feelings of
guilt that would plague me after my actions. It felt like
another unfair fact of life. In my mind, no one who
had ever hurt me felt guilty. That was something I
couldn't possibly know.

I would like to insert a thought here. As
children grow up, they change. The older they get, the
more they will act out the things they've seen in their
environment. A baby will believe the lies that their
parents tell them for a little while. As they get older,
however, the "do as I say and not as I do" becomes
ineffective. We cannot be good parents if we allow
our children to grow up in a chaotic environment.

Sometimes, the alternatives may not seem all
that great. I've seen people who are involved in
abusive relationships stay together because of
children. I've seen them stay together because of a
mortgage or a car note, for financial security, or for
sex - as awful as that may sound. The point is:
sometimes the person you love doesn't always love
you back. To stay in situations that are harmful to you
and to the children that God has given you
stewardship over is like committing spiritual suicide.

There are those of you who will read this book and feel that your course is already set, and like you can't do any better. Your circumstances may tell you that you are trapped. The devil is a liar. There are five things I learned the hard way:

1. Sometimes it's easier to be alone.
2. Sometimes it's better to start over with nothing.
3. Never trade your peace for financial security.
4. Children remember what you wish they would forget.
5. Actions or the lack thereof, matter.

The horrible fact is that verbal, physical and sexual abuse is more prevalent than any studies will ever be able to show. For every person who speaks up, there are at least 3 who will not.

You should never be willing to trade your safety for companionship. It's not easy to be alone or to walk away from relationships you have built your dreams upon, but it's a lot harder to wonder when a fight might end a life. It's harder to wonder what the far-reaching effect of your abusive relationship may be on your children and grandchildren, even if you aren't there to see it firsthand.

Physically abusive relationships were normal, common even, for me, my mother before me, and her mother before her. I actually didn't know *anyone*, neither male nor female, personally who had not been either a victim of, or a victimizer by way of, physical abuse. That speaks volumes!

~Chapter 9~
You Are So Beautiful To Me

During the most stressful years of my life, my mom could not be there. Very early on, she began battling a drug and alcohol problem that would remain ongoing to this very day.

My mind goes back to one summer when I was around seven or eight years old. I had gone to Little Rock for a summer break. After I had been there awhile, a fight arose between my mother and my stepfather. It was horrific for me to watch, so I went and grabbed my grandfather's shotgun. I aimed it at my stepfather and tried to shoot him, but I had forgotten how to take the safety off so the trigger would work. Both of them were racing to get to me before I figured it out. By the time I found the safety, my mom had made it to me and wrestled the gun from me. That traumatized all of us, and a few weeks later, they took me back to Warren.

When we got to Warren, we found my grandmother at her boyfriend's house. After we'd been there awhile, I found out they intended to leave me there, I cried until it hurt. I screamed, kicked and threw a fit. Finally, my mother said she was going to stay, but that she needed to take our clothes to my grandmother's house. She left me with my grandmother, promising to come right back. I had no reason to doubt that we would all troop back over to my grandmother's house together later that evening. My grandmother knew she was lying but went along with it, thinking to ease my mother's departure.

I remember hearing them talk; my grandmother told my mother to take me with her because I didn't want to stay with her. She seemed hurt by my desire to be with my mother. I suppose she felt unappreciated. She had always been there for me. She wasn't a "summer mother", but was there year round. I heard something else in her voice too. It wasn't until adulthood that I distinguished it. She wanted my mother to grow up and *act* like a mother. It was, after all, her responsibility to take care of her children. There was also a hint of guilt behind my grandmother's voice. Maybe she was seeing herself in my mother and was feeling some regret. Still, I know she wanted my mother to be better than she was.

I sat on the couch and waited. I waited and waited some more. That same day, at that very hour, I remember Luke and Laura from General Hospital were getting married. Their wedding song was *You Are So Beautiful to Me*. That became my theme song which portrayed my pain and disappointment with my mother. I had always thought she was beautiful, if elusive, even to me. To me, it was the perfect song to play as I waited on my beautiful mother to come back. I was excited that I could again have both my mother and grandmother together in the same place.

Finally, after waiting for hours, I begged my grandmother to let me walk to our house to see if she was there. She didn't have the heart to tell me she was not there. In fact, they had been gone long enough to make it back to Little Rock. I half ran and half skipped all the way home. A part of me was afraid that she was not there. Another side of me wanted to believe she would be there waiting on me. I was scared and excited at the same time. I have not, since that time, felt how powerful the emotional duality of human nature can be. The fear and expectation mingled keenly to create something I cannot describe though I remember it and still feel it as if it were just yesterday.

When I walked into the house and found that she was not there, the emptiness of the house was amplified in my heart. Some part of me shriveled up and died. I wanted to die along with it. I called her name and diligently searched for her. I screamed "Mama!" repeatedly, as if my screaming and looking would yield some kind of result! She was gone; she had left me again. I was so hurt that I sank along with my heart. Tears flooded my eyes as if they were connected to some well of anguish. They just would not stop coming. I can't remember ever hurting like that before that time nor since. The first time I wrote this section, I had to put down the pencil and allow myself to grieve. Of all the memories this book entails, this is one is by far most painful! The first time I went through this section, I cried nearly an hour though it happened more than twenty years ago. Now, going through it a final time, I still find that I had to pause because of a few new tears that welled up in my eyes.

That was the day optimism died in me. I learned never to expect anything good, not when it concerned my family. Pessimism was birthed in me that day. It hurt too much to expect something good and then not receive it. Disappointment was too painful for me to bear. I would try to model my life and my thoughts, from that point, in such a way that disappointment would never visit me again.

Even now, the memory of that day still hurts. It's one of the few memories in this book that I dread the public knowing and asking me about. I love my mother and she is very special to me, but there was a time when I could barely stand to be around her. Even then though, the child in me still cried out for her. I know she made the decision to allow my grandmother to raise me for many reasons, the least of which was for my own safety. She was trying to protect me and help my grandmother out. She thought I would be better off without her. She did love me, but she failed to realize that I needed her presence more than anything else. Of course, when I look at her story, mine seems to pale in comparison. She went through so much more than I, and like me, my mother didn't know what to feel or what to do with herself. She, like me, tried to embrace detachment and feel nothing.

My mother was raped by her uncle, my grandmother's brother, and was left naked on side of the road. When she did make it home, she told her mother. That same uncle, when confronted, denied it and swore on his very life that my mother was lying. A short time later, he died in a car accident.

My mother was almost overdosed and killed by her own husband when she caught him shooting up in their bathroom. She survived that, but she later got hooked on Valium after he shot her in her back and in her side. Her drug problem only exacerbated from there. My mom suffered from seizures. She has been beaten by almost every man she has ever been with. I know my mom loved me more than she could say, but she had precious little control over her own life and most certainly couldn't take care of a little girl. As an adult, and as God has shown me, I realize that she made the best decision she could have made under those circumstances. Sometimes, there are not a lot of options in life, and the ones we have are not always wonderful. She faced that time with as much courage as she could muster. Living with my grandmother was one of the things God used to help me avoid being entangled with some of the terrible things Little Rock would have certainly held in store for me. Being with my grandmother also gave my mother and grandmother some common ground that had been missing for years.

I don't believe that my mother ever *felt* truly loved by my grandmother. However, I know that my grandmother loved my mother very much. She was disappointed in her. She wanted her to succeed in all the places she had failed. What my grandmother didn't realize is that she had not shown my mother *how* to succeed. My mother had begun life in a bad environment. She had nearly killed three people before she was 21 years old. She'd been forced to protect my grandmother from an abusive boyfriend that was about to kill her mother. She had been exposed to the humiliation of molestation by one of my grandmother's boyfriends. How *could* she succeed with that kind of past, without God and without a mother who was able to teach and protect her?

My mother had grown up afraid, learning to protect herself in the only way she knew... violently. Her survival instinct had necessarily turned on, but it didn't turn off, partly because dangers never seemed to cease for her. Because it stayed "on" so long, it became dull and ineffective. The more she tried to protect herself and those she loved, the worse things seemed to get. Her simple solution would have been to stop the madness and be alone with her children for a little while. She couldn't see the simple solution, just as many people who are living in dire straits do not.

I learned to appreciate my mother's efforts. Through all the years, and, even with all our mistakes toward each other, she is still just as beautiful to me now as she was to the little girl who once sat waiting for her return while watching Luke and Laura get married on *General Hospital*.

~Chapter 10~
And Death Did Touch My Life

In the prime of my childhood, at the age of fifteen years old, I had a son. Montario, who was quickly nicknamed Tario by his dad, was a healthy and beautiful baby boy. The labor was uneventful and I knew that I wanted a few more children.

At the age of sixteen, I had my second son, Tyrail. He came one month early and was born with liver failure. The idea of a possible future cesarean section was so heinous to me then that I decided to let them tie my fallopian tubes. Little did I know then that I was making a mistake that I would regret all the days of my life. I was making an adult decision based on fear and without all the facts.

Tyrail was born on May 19, 1992 and died on June 19, 1992. He suffered a lot in his little time here on earth. When he died, a part of me died with him. Had I known my son would die, never in a million years would I have agreed to get my tubes tied. Nevertheless, I nearly bled to death after I had him. I was very weak. I stayed in the hospital in Warren for almost two weeks, while my son was being treated in a hospital in Little Rock. It was unbearable to be without him. I could hardly remember what he looked like. I just knew he was special to me. From conception to birth, he'd had a calming effect on me. That time was very short lived.

At the time of my son's death, I had never experienced the loss of someone extremely close to me to die. Death of a loved one brings such an agonizing sorrow. Unlike any other cruelty upon the earth, death does not give up what it claims for itself.

There is no tomorrow with death. It marks the end of relationships here upon the earth. There are no more phone calls or visits. There is no more holding, hugging or cuddling. There are no more opportunities to fight or to make up. All death leaves behind are memories or regrets (or both) for the one who is left unless they know the Lord. Even then, the loss can be nearly unbearable.

A short time after the death of my second-born, my stepfather died too. A year or so later, my real dad, James York, died. During that time, my grandmother's boyfriend, also like a dad, had suffered a stroke and was sick. I felt fatherless. I guess in all actuality I was. By the time my stepfather died, I was not very close with him anymore. For some reason, that still did not take the sting away from knowing he was permanently gone. When my biological dad died, I felt cheated. I did not know him as well as I would have liked to know him. I didn't know if he loved me. I didn't know what he thought when I was born. I didn't know anything. In my mind, I wanted to believe he loved me, but his absence had shown me differently.

Covering up my feelings had become habitual in the life that was living me. I thought that covering them was easier than facing them. Grief was no less real for me than for anyone else, but since I did not know how to grieve, so I decided to feel nothing. Death, though, is permanent and you can only hide your pain for so long. Death has a way of forcing you to be honest with yourself.

In 1998, I lost my grandmother to cancer. Later on that same year, I lost my grandfather. Those were tremendous losses to both my mother and me.

My grandmother had raised me. She was a foundation for me. She had kept me grounded and helped me to keep my focus in some very turbulent times. Losing my grandmother caused me to stop and take inventory of my life. I was so full of sorrow and regret! It was at that time that I realized the importance of showing love to those around me. I realized it, but it would be many years later before I would be able to put it into action.

~Chapter 11~
Inconvenience of a Convenient Marriage

With my grandmother gone, I felt unstable and off balance. I had no one to run to, no one to accept me unconditionally. I felt that I had lost the only guaranteed love I'd had. I was desperate for some kind of stability again. I needed someone to make me feel loved. Who better than the current man in my life?

I became Mrs. Elias Duncan on January 1, 1999. It was a convenient marriage. He was stable and kind. He actually reminded me of my grandmother in many ways. He was funny in an off-the-wall kind of way. He was a hard worker. He treated me with respect and I loved him for that.

After moving to his hometown, the relationship between me and my night in shining armor began to change. I'm sure now that he was trying to protect me from the opinions of people, but I wasn't mature enough to see that then. It seemed to me that he was trying to control me. I did what I had been doing most of my life when that happened. I rebelled. I chose to rebel against a man who treated me like a princess. Everything he told me *not* to do I did, because I didn't understand his reasoning.

Our marriage really began to go bad when his family involved themselves in our relationship. It seemed I could do nothing right by them. I had entered into marriage with every good intention. I had decided never to cheat or lie to him. I wanted to try doing something right. Nevertheless, good intentions are just those... intentions.

After being married for a little while, things went sour fast. I was tired of "being good" and yet still be accused of doing things I wasn't doing. To me, I saw no reason to continue trying to be a good wife. My efforts were going unrecognized. That was enough for my search for acceptance to begin all over again.

I don't condone any facet, form, or degree of adultery, whether in actions or thoughts. I don't condone fornication either. They are sins that destroy marriages, families, self-esteem and even financial and possibly bodily health. These particular sins destroyed many of my own dreams and nearly ruined my life. It took God to bring restoration to me, and to Elias.

I began to cheat on my husband. I justified myself by believing it didn't really matter whether I did or didn't commit adultery. It seemed that I wasn't going to be accepted whether I did good or bad. I was rejected no matter what I did. To my way of thinking, no one really approved of me anyway. I was tired of trying to get approval, so, I rebelled, even against my better judgment. I began to act like what people seemed to think I was. What more was there for me to do? There were many more options than I knew, and unfortunately, my ignorance hurt a lot of people.

My own debilitations were the primary reasons my marriage ended. Once I began to cheat on Elias, it seemed nearly impossible to stop. I felt trapped again because I had once more given myself over to a life that kept me in bondage. I continued on this path for years, at least until God's divine intervention was manifested in my life.

~Chapter 12~
Enter the Christ

In January 2001, Jesus Christ changed my life. I had been living in Louisiana for almost 2 years with my second husband, Elias. My best friend, Rachelle, was affiliated with a Prophetess named Marguerite from Baton Rouge, LA. They often talked on the phone. I had heard many great things about Miss Marguerite, though we had never met each other.

The entire week before I met Jesus and accepted Him as my Savior, I had been feeling out of sorts. I'd felt very anxious and tired. Nothing was making me happy. No matter how much money I spent, or how many shoes (my favorite indulgence) I purchased, I couldn't shake the blues. I had finally lost my desire to shop – which was unheard of at that point in my life.

On that Wednesday, I decided to visit Rachelle. She had a nice, quiet apartment. I loved visiting with her because she was always a lot of fun to be around. However, I didn't find any relief there either. After I had been at her house for a few minutes, the phone rang. It was Miss Marguerite.

Reflecting back on that night, it seemed I knew that my life needed to and would soon change somehow. Before I left my house, I was sure that *something* was coming, and because I had learned not to expect anything good, I expected something bad would happen.

When I found out that Rachelle was on the phone with Miss Marguerite, I was in a hurry to leave. I don't know why I rushed out of her apartment in such a hurry… perhaps it was because the enemy knew that if I had stayed, salvation would have found me there. I usually would have waited for Rachelle to get off the phone, but not that night. I suppose the devil knew that the time I'd spent living for him was coming to a close. In his last ditch effort, he was compelling me to go home and get away from that "spiritual" stuff. Even so, God will never be outdone! When *He* wants you, there is nothing Satan can do about it! I found out quickly that once your appointed time has come for certain change, you can't outrun it. A person can reject it, but can never outrun it. God is good like that!

As Rachelle talked on the phone, I waved goodbye and signaled that I was going home. Before I was home a full one minute, the phone was ringing. It was Rachelle and she had Miss Marguerite on the other line. The Prophetess had been talking to Rachelle about a friend of hers who was troubled. Rachelle knew I was the one whom Miss Marguerite spoke of, so she called to inform me that Miss Marguerite had a word for me from God. I came very close to not answering the phone. Even when I did, I *still* didn't want a word from a prophetess. Of course, I'm not a rude person by nature, even when I want to be. Being rude was a trait I never mastered, at least not outside of extreme anger. I might *think* a million and one things, but I really do hate to hurt anyone's feelings… so, I indulged Miss Marguerite and listened to what she had to say.

Before she started, she had given me fair warning. She asked if I wanted to have the conversation in private. I guess the part of me that was full of unbelief didn't think God really had anything to say to me now, if, in fact, He was speaking at all. I felt like I was one of the worst people on the planet. Never mind that I had heard Him speak to me before. Never mind that He made promises to me as a child in a heathen family. I lost my belief in His words to me as I had lost everything else. So, I told Miss Marguerite she could speak freely in front of Rachelle. I told Rachelle "everything", so why should I be ashamed of anything? I regretted that decision almost immediately; I *was* ashamed of *plenty* things. Those would be the things that God would discuss with me that night through an unknown prophetess in front of my best friend.

As she began to speak to me, I swiftly realized that she was definitely hearing God. She told me that God had been with me my whole life. She dealt with some things from my past, present and future. In fact, she told me that God said there was a tragedy coming in three days if I did not surrender my life. I knew it had to be true because I had been feeling it all week long.

She dealt with the pain and frustration I'd harbored over what I endured as a child. She went so far into the private depths of my life that I couldn't deny God's love for me any longer. Certainly, I knew that He not only loved me, but that He was also trying to protect me.

As the conversation progressed, I realized that I wanted God more than anything. I wanted Jesus Christ to be my Lord and Savior and told her as much. She prayed with me and told me to be sure to make it to church on that coming Sunday. She explained the importance of going to church and getting that strength from other believers.

After I got off the phone with them, I wept the whole while I prayed to God. I spent hours with Him, appreciating His love and acceptance of me. I had always known, though I don't know *how* I knew, how to talk to God. That night, it seemed as if He was truly mine. In my desperation, I vowed never to let go of Him. In my ignorance, I begged Him never to let go of me. And in the depths of my pain, a relationship with God was formed that would be the only constant in my life for years to come.

I have never been a morning person, but on that next Sunday morning, I was up and ready in plenty of time to get to where I was going... Hope United Methodist Church. Under the leadership of Pastor Jackie Holmes, Hope was the place I gained a renewed hope for my future, and where my walk with Christ began.

No End in Sight

I was never simplistic in my thinking. To the contrary, I was always one to over-think a situation and over-analyze *all* the solutions. For the first time in my life, on that night, I simply accepted Christ into my heart. I let go of myself and allowed God to have full control over my life. I cannot say that the journey has always been easy, but everything that I have gone through was a small price to pay in comparison to all that I received in my Father.

I had always known, even from the age of eight years old, that God had a plan for my life. For the most part of my childhood, I'd always somehow managed to believe that God was going to turn my shame away, that He would make me into someone great. However, as I got older, that faith wavered; by the time the night arrived when God moved to do what I had believed from childhood, it seemed more like fantasy than reality. In those long years between eight and twenty-five, my faith had been based solely upon a voice I'd heard during the most traumatic times in my life. I was starting to feel foolish. Nevertheless, God's timing is perfect. He, by Himself, pulled me through some things that only He could. He started me on another path that night, one that would sometimes hurt because of the straightness by which a person must walk when they walk with the Lord. The path was narrow then, and still is – and long, but the benefits on the path are worth the trials.

I wish I could say that once I received salvation, my struggles were over, yet my problems were far from over. Though my relationship with God was solidified through salvation, deliverance and healing had to come about. Miss Marguerite, in her wisdom, didn't choose to share the trials I would soon face. No one told me about the constant battle that would wage between my flesh and my spirit. Neither did anyone tell me that I would still have to go back and face those skeletons in my closet, taking back their power over me. I assumed that God would do all those things for me. I was in for a big shock! I was about to see what things I had to suffer for His name's sake. Though I was a baby learning to walk like my heavenly Father, I was about to do more falling than walking for a long while. Notwithstanding, I was also about to discover hidden strengths inside myself.

I've Fallen and Need Help Getting Up

At first, I was progressing well. I taught my first Bible studies in May of 2001, only four months after salvation. I preached my first sermon on July 29, 2001, only six months after salvation. I had a heart to do ministry work. I was zealous and bold for the Lord. Even so, I quickly found out that God was after my reserves. He was after my harbored hurts. Most times, harbored hurts are discovered through a sifting process. When they're buried as deeply as mine were, sifting must take place.

After some time, my life came under attack. As Satan began to assault my life, I became weak. My marriage was the first thing that suffered. Once again, I found myself hating that I was married. I began to despise my husband for no apparent reason. I felt abandoned again. Because Elias would not support me in the way that *I* wanted, the marriage was coming apart at the seams. Soon, I was back to my old ways... I was having adulterous affairs... with married preachers!

I'm certain that some of you who are reading this book are surprised that I would ever admit to being an adulterer while being in ministry, and especially with other married preachers. Not everyone will want to hear this truth. If you are one of those people, you might want to put this book down right now. The truth makes us free. We overcome the devil by the blood of the Lamb and the words of our testimonies. People in the world cannot hide their sins and neither should people in the church try to hide their sins. Honesty destroys hypocrisy.

During my weaker moments, I slept with three married pastors. All of them had successful ministries. I believed I was in love with one of them. Truly, I did love him deeply, or as deeply as sin will allow you to go. We had something of an ethereal relationship in some ways, though in reality, it was a spiritual disaster. Though it seemed delicate and otherworldly, it was actually a nightmare waiting to happen. It was a sinful fantasy and it cost me more than I ever wanted to pay. It was perverse and harmful.

When I would go out to preach, God would use me mightily to minister healing, deliverance and restoration to others. Still, I saw no change in my own life. I felt powerless to do anything about my own issues. I felt that I needed someone to lay hands on *me* too! I needed someone to show me the way to actually *live* free. The problem with that was no one I knew at that time lived holy. They all had issues, just like I did. Though very few of us wrestled with the same problem in details, all the ministers I knew struggled in the area of self-control. Deliverance never happened like I wanted it to – by some holy person laying hands on me. Somehow, I knew it would be a bit more difficult for me, as most things were.

Of all the things I struggled with, fornication and adultery seemed to stick with me more than all my other issues. They were definitely strongholds of old in my life, but ones I was determined to beat. For me, they were rooted in overindulgence and an insatiable hunger for love.

The adulterous affair with the first pastor was something I did out of spite. I wasn't attracted to him. It was pure rebellion (that sin that's just like witchcraft)! False accusations made me curious about him. The fact that two other women preachers were mad enough to fight me over him when nothing had happened between us only made me the more curious. Though my old nature was dead in Christ, I hadn't changed my mindset. I was still spiteful and vengeful. The old person had reared her ugly head.

The second affair was the one in which the spirit of perversion came upon me the strongest. I deceived myself into believing it was okay because his wife treated him bad. I cannot blame him for my deception. It wasn't his fault alone. I *wanted* to believe his lies. I wanted to believe the lies of the enemy. I was dying on the inside. The decay in my spirit was rottenness to my bones. My mind was troubled all the time. My days were spent no more in prayer for deliverance from the relationship, but in prayer that he could be set free from a marriage he'd sworn he didn't want. My heart was being toyed with, but not as much by him as by the devil.

From the first moment that I met him, the Spirit of God was telling me to run. Yet, my husband believed in him as a man of God and wanted to fellowship with him. I can't say that God doesn't bring warning. He has never let anything come upon me while I am unaware. He has always warned me ahead of time.

I fell headlong into the trap of feeling sorry for this preacher. I thought I could pray for and minister to him. I wanted to help him because I couldn't stand that miserable look on his face. He was my "friend" and I was determined to see him through his hard time.

Before we began to sleep together, my new pastor at that time warned me by the Spirit that it was about to happen. He told me it would happen three times if we weren't careful, but never again, no matter what we did. However, this *same* pastor told me that God would give him, a married pastor, to me, a still married minister myself, if we did things "right". My pastor would tell me that this man really loved me and that God had shown him this or that concerning the situations I would often find myself in with the married pastor.

Truly, this man and I slept together three times like spoken to me and never again. Those three months of a perverse relationship nearly cost me my life: for three months of what I thought was pleasure, I paid with three years of pain. I wanted to die and those suicidal thoughts came rushing back upon me, not because he was so great and hard for me to let go of, but because suicide was already a temptation for me. Suicide was always my easy answer, though my attempts to carry it out would never work.

I told my husband about the affair, not that I really had to. Elias was gifted, but he would never address a situation head on unless he was forced to face it. He hated being wrong and never trusted his spiritual gifts. After telling my husband, and because of the confrontation that ensued, the relationship between this married pastor and I ceased for a long while.

A year later, I failed another trial with another married pastor. At this point, my marriage was over all but the physical separation. The side of me that knew divorce was wrong wanted to stay in the relationship. The side of me that felt trapped wanted out.

I can't say that I walked into this one-night stand type of relationship with the third married pastor in ignorance. I knew what I was doing was wrong. Still, I felt compelled to do it anyway. He was a prophet. I couldn't deny his gift. I knew he was anointed for a purpose, but I also knew he was weak in his flesh. He talked about all these ways he could help me if he were to become my pastor and the whole time I knew he would sleep with me. In order to prove myself right, and to discredit him in my own mind, I purposely disobeyed God. I suppose I really only wanted to protect myself from caring about him too much. Perversion is the craziest thing. It actually sounds right until God shows you the light. To me, the end (determining his motives) justified the means (going to be alone with him in a hotel 3 hours from home.)

In all reality, I was still seeking someone who loved me and not necessarily only my body. It used to hurt me so much to meet someone I thought was great, but to see them oogling me. I hated it. It made me feel cheap and kept me captive to my past. I found that I still hated men. Even though I professed salvation, to me, men were my issue. All of them were dirty and all of them were only out for what they could get. All of them together were worth less than a penny to me.

Deliverance, Sometimes Unwanted

At the height of my perverted deception, God used a friend to bring truth into my life in a way that I couldn't argue back. She let me borrow a VHS tape by T.D. Jakes called *Subtle Deceit*. As I watched the videotape that night, God began to use T.D. Jakes to help me see the truth. Reality began to set in. That was a glimpse into freedom for me. I began to let go of the men. I thought I had surely been completely delivered... little did I know, total deliverance was still a long way off.

God had so much work to do on me! Through it all, I continued to pray, even when my prayers didn't line up with the Word of God. I continued to read the Bible, though I wasn't walking very much of it out. I continued to preach for a long while and saw God do great things. Nevertheless, I was still filled with hate. I was still rebellious. I was still filled with shame. My thoughts were still full of perversion. I had a long way to go and through it all, I had to continue in a marriage that I didn't want anymore.

Finally, Elias and I separated in March of 2004. I prayed and prayed over this marriage. I wanted out. God eventually spoke to me. He told me that He could salvage my marriage. He said that if I chose to walk out of it, I would go through some very hard things for three years. He told me I would face financial difficulties. He told me about the struggles it would cause for me in ministry. He told me about everything that was about to befall me. I wasn't really listening like I should have. To me, I had been given a license to leave. In reality, it *wasn't* a license to leave. It was a warning not to.

True to the word of the Lord, it would be three years before the divorce would be final. In those three years, my heart was broken more than once. I faced extreme poverty. I went from always being independent to having to live with other people when I knew didn't want me at their house. I was mistreated more times by more people in the church than I would ever want to put on paper. I went through it over and over again in those three years.

Sometimes, I did stop to wonder if I'd made a mistake, though this is the first time I've ever admitted it.

My convenient marriage had turned into an inconvenient marriage. The separation was even *more* inconvenient. Still, I had come to a point where I would have decided death was a fate better than being trapped in the marriage I was in. I do want to say that Elias was not the sole reason I didn't want to be in the relationship anymore. He wasn't even a fraction of a percent of the reason. It was all a demonic attack, selfishness and preconceived notions. All of those negative feelings were temporary, though to me they felt permanent at that time. I made a permanent decision based upon emotions, oppression and deception. We, as people, do that all too often. *When* we do, catastrophe is always the outcome. When perverse desires and fleshly lusts are the driving desires in our lives, shipwreck happens. There is no stopping it. The things that come from the devil always take us through hell. It's a principle that we cannot change. What comes from the devil goes back to him. What comes from God goes back to Him.

My ex-husband is a great man. He deserves only the best. He went through a lot trying to love me, but he had no idea what he was up against. I thank God that we are still friends and can speak to one another. We can still enjoy conversation together. After all the pain I caused him, only God could do that.

No one told me the whole truth about salvation. I often feel that I would have fared much better if I had known about the forces of the enemy that would come against me. I blindly fought many

67

battles and still have many more to fight. I would like to say that I have won most of my battles, but that would be a lie. I lost many battles in the beginning. It took me a little while to catch on.

~Chapter 13~
Preach, Pray and Pretend

As my personal struggles continued, my ability to pretend began to slip away. I left Hope United Methodist Church in August 2002. I began to go to New Nation Evangelistic Assembly. It was a big change for me. It was like transcending worlds. This pastor was more personal with his members. It seemed everyone in the church had been called to the five-fold ministry. It was a church full of preachers.

My new pastor quickly became like a brother to me. He was a friend and soon became a colleague at work. He walks in the office of a prophet. In many ways, being around him everyday ended my pretense. He was often very hard on me. I guess even then, he could see where God was taking me. He was continually pushing and prying. It irked me like crazy.

Through the prayers of the saints and because I was under leadership that required much more accountability, God was able to lead me to true deliverance in many areas of my life. It still took me more than three years to get free from certain perversions in my mind. Even so, freedom by any means is not free. It takes work and diligence.

No matter how bad it got, God kept on using me for His glory. He had invested something wonderful in me. God had birthed impartiality in me. In that one area, there has never been any doubt in my mind as to whether or not God was pleased. No matter if the Word convicts, admonishes or edifies, I have always been and always will be committed to telling the unadulterated truth, even if it uncovers me before the people.

From the first moment of salvation until now, I have been diligent in the Word of God. Throughout many nights, I kept my nose in the Bible. Sometimes, I read and studied until I was blue in the face. Studying has its rewards. God revealed many mysteries to me. God opened many revelations to me also.

Though I studied extensively, I rarely ever prayed the way I should have. I would talk to God all the time, but rarely did I go down on my knees to humbly seek out a deeper and more intimate relationship with Him. My conversations with Him were very informal and irregular. Today I understand the importance of getting on your knees... God showed me the hard way.

Through heartache, I learned to pray and cry before God. Through humiliation, I learned to bow before God. I learned to praise Him through my lack and worship Him in my overflow.

There have been times when I've had to speak to God while choking back sobs. I often praised Him with a lump in my throat that I could not swallow. I've sung until I cried. I then sang until I stopped crying. I have sometimes been so angry that it was all I could do not to curse while explaining my side of things to God. I have occasionally accused Him of being unfair and of not loving me enough. I have sometimes tried to manipulate God in my prayers by saying, "Well, if you love me..." or "If you care about me at all..." I've come to God in fear and I've come to Him in faith. All of it worked together for my good. It taught me how to come to Him. Through trial and error, I learned what I should pray. I learned what was ineffective with God and what actually brought swift answers. I also learned that in His sovereignty, He has the right to deny me some things and to delay those things that He has promised. He cannot be manipulated. He cannot be rushed. He cannot be commanded. *He must be entreated.* He must be given control over a situation before He will move in it. He is at all times a gentleman and will not take from you what you will not give. Does that sound contrary?

God ministered something to me in the midst of one of my trials! He taught me that trials and storms are not to wrench certain things away from us, but that some of them are to make us want to let them go. Once a person really wants to get rid of something, it takes God no time to move it. Yet, we are known to be what many call "Indian-givers". We will give our issues to Him and then take them back. We are sometimes double-minded and unstable. Therefore, God allows certain things to happen to us that the false gods we put before Him may be shown up and removed from our lives.

Human nature dictates that we hold tightly to the things we love. More than one person has been guilty of squeezing the life out of a beloved thing. For instance, as long as I love sex outside of marriage, I won't stop sinning in adultery or fornication, even if only in my thought life. I might leave the act, but not the thought. I might no longer practice it, but I may yet take pleasure in someone else doing it. God, in His infinite mercy, and in order to keep and perfect us, will allow things to happen so that what we once loved will hurt us enough to destroy the love that ties us to whatever it is.

For years, I pretended to be something I wasn't. Most people in the churches I went to weren't used to unbridled honesty. Some things were not to be said or admitted publicly. Some issues were only for other preachers to help me with. Some stuff was expected to remain between God and myself. I was expected to put on my game face before the world and paint a picture that didn't line up with what I was living, one that couldn't be further from the truth. I was expected to hold it together when I felt like I might die. I was expected to get it together when it was apparent that I didn't know how. I was expected to "suck it up" when the pain was so great that I thought I'd die of a broken heart. I was expected to be strong when in reality I was weak. A heavy burden was placed upon me, as often is the case when wounded ministers are required to bleed silently behind the pulpit. Part of this expectation comes from ministers, but the other part of it comes from the congregation that believes all preachers do, or should, have it all together. I won't get into that now. That is another book. Suffice to say, no one has everything all together. Yet, there are certain issues that should never be present behind the pulpit.

In those times, I asked God why He had called me to go into ministry. He finally showed me that He needed someone who was not afraid to be transparent, to show faults along with strengths to the world. God is not into tickling itching ears and portraying falsities to a dying world. He deals only in truth because anything won by a lie won't survive the truth. If our converts and our church memberships cannot stand in the fires of truth, they aren't really converts at all. They are membership, which means nothing on the day each of us must stand before the Judgment Seat of Christ.

I was taught how and encouraged to pretend, but God told me that truth was the way. I was taught the right prayers, but God showed me the heart prayers. I was taught how to exhort the people, but God had to show me how to exhort myself. Everything that I was taught by man had purpose, but it was the things that God taught me which will last throughout eternity.

A pastor warned me that writing this book would cause some people involved in ministry to hate me. Well, I've been hated before and I lived through it. It does not matter to me who hates the truth. God loves it and I plan to tell it all.

I was also admonished that I could destroy people's faith in the Church if I wrote and published this book. Well, to that I say, people should have faith in God and not the Church. The people *are* the Church. *Jesus Christ* is our Savior. We put our trust in Him and Him alone. We cannot put trust in flesh. As long as we teach people to trust fleshly man and to exalt fleshly man, people will be offended by the hypocrisy of man long before any truth is ever read from this book.

I was told that people can't handle too much truth. My question is, "What is too much?" In John 14: 6, Jesus said, *"...I am the way, the truth, and the life: no man cometh unto the Father, but by me."*

It is only through truth that people find relationship with the Father. It's not possible to fake your way into heaven. It is by truth that yokes of bondage are destroyed and people are changed forever. It is by truth that we approach our Father. It is by truth even that we worship Him. Jesus told the woman at Jacob's well in John chapter 4, verse 24: *"God is a Spirit: and they that worship him must worship him in spirit and in truth."*

In John 8:32, Jesus told the Jews that believed: *"And ye shall know the truth, and the truth shall make you free."* In Ephesians 6:14, as Paul is describing the armor of God, he says this: *"Stand therefore, having your loins girt about with truth..."*

Where did the pretending come from? Jesus never pretended. The word, *pretend,* comes from the same word as *pretense,* which is another word for lie... the very thing God says He hates. Yet, in pulpits all over the world, people are pretending while claiming to have the answers for hurting people. That's like playing nurse with a dying person. It's unfair and ineffective.

If God, desiring to make us more like Him, cannot lie, why do we work so hard at lying? Lying isn't just what we say, but it's also what we do. Thankfully, I have come to a place where my reputation isn't important enough for me to pretend. I am who I am, and where I am. I have to give an account to God for what I do. I don't need to uphold a standard by pretense, but in truth.

There are very few people who understand how exposing these facts from behind the pulpit can be beneficial. Some believe that what I'm sharing could possibly destroy the Body of Christ at large. I don't want to, nor do I have the power to, actually destroy the church. I do, however, want to destroy the lies that make the work of the church ineffective.

It is time for us as ministers to be who we say we are. If the blind can't lead the blind, then certainly a liar can't teach the ways of truth.

~Chapter 14~
Knowing Him as Father

Most of my life, I felt worthless, with the exception of how quickly I learned in the academic arena. Though I never admitted it, growing up in a broken and dysfunctional family made life hard for me. No matter what man came into my mother's and grandmother's lives, I never forgot the absence of my biological father. I never stopped missing him. I don't think any man could have ever made me stop missing him. Regardless of who loved me, I craved the love of my father badly. I grew up without a lot of things, but the thing I desired most was the love of James York, the man whose blood coursed through my veins.

In 2004, I met my oldest sister, Renea, for the first time. It was a strange sensation seeing her. She looks like the female version of our father. She even speaks like him. As I grew closer to her, she told me many things about our heritage. She had the fortunate opportunity to know about our father and his family. Our father, for the majority of her life, raised her. He had taught her things, spanked her when she was mischievous, and been there when she first began to date. She had all the things I'd never received from our dad and knowing that left a tremendous hurt inside me. I felt as if she had what I was denied; that was so unfair to me! I often pondered how much we looked alike and how many character flaws we have in common... yet, he found time for her and not for me. That was mind boggling to me. It was like a slap in the face, though I never took it out on her. Still, I was very jealous. I would have gladly traded almost anything to have had even a spanking from my real father. Instead, all I had were six unspectacular memories, brief encounters with a man that I should have known intimately.

It was only recently that my mother shared some things pertaining to my father with me. He had kept me quite often when I was a baby. He diapered and fed me from time to time. He fussed over me, his baldheaded baby girl. He thought I was one of the most beautiful things he had ever seen. For me to finally hear the things he'd said when I was born was like waiting to exhale. Even then, it was a bittersweet moment. I still longed to hear those words myself. His absence from my life, however painful, set the stage for me to learn how to love God as Father.

One night, I was reading a passage out of a book. What I read ministered to me and set me free in my thinking in many ways. The author spoke of knowing God as Father. As I read the characteristics the author had attributed to God, I realized that He is indeed a loving Father and a concerned Creator. That revelation made me go back to my Bible with a fresh perspective.

Looking over my favorite passages of scripture and gaining new insight to the ones I'd often passed over, I realized that God is qualified to be Father because He is Creator. No one made Him create man. He did it for His own great purposes. God, in His own infinite wisdom, mercy and love, desired people for His inheritance. He wanted to love us and for us to love Him. He wanted all humanity to know that we are here by His choice. He wanted fellowship and sweet communion with us, His people, fashioned from dirt by His hands. So awesome was His great love for us that He sacrificed His only begotten Son.

As I endeavored to accept God as my all-sufficient Father, I found that my prayer life was a crucial part of building a relationship with the Father of all creation. God knows all things. Nothing surprises Him or takes Him off guard. Still, His heart beats for us to walk and talk with Him. He wants us to run to Him when we are hurt, disappointed, tired or depressed. He wants us to rejoice with Him when we are happy and excited. He wants to be our shoulder to cry on and our comforter throughout all ages. No different from you, God wants your attention. Slowly I began to realize that God, like we people, wants affection.

As I began to accept the love of God and as I allowed Him to saturate me in His love, I also grew in my ability to trust Him. I came to the realization that I can trust God with my hurts, my wrongs, my downfalls and my emotions. I found out that I could trust Him with my life. After all, what else are dads for? They carefully watch over their children, guarding and protecting them with all diligence. Good dads are more than willing to lay down their lives for their children. Dads train their children to make right decisions and to take care of business in excellence. Dads discipline their children for bad decisions. Most of all, dads support their children, always loving them unconditionally. God does all of this for each of His children and more. He is always there to forgive, to cleanse, to clarify, to rectify and to help His children. He always loves in all circumstances. He never forsakes and never turns away from those that belong to Him.

I can so easily picture a father watching his child take their first breath and cry their first cry. That same father is there when the child takes that first step and falls. That same father is there the first time the child drives, goes on a date, falls in love or ends up with a broken heart. That same father walks his daughter down the aisle at her wedding, or gives his son "the talk" before he gets married. God is that same Father. He knew us before birth and was with us even then. He will be there in death and beyond.

It wasn't easy for me to know how to respond to God in His role as Father. His role as Master was simple. I had to obey. His role as Provider was simple. I had to ask. His role as Healer was simple. I had to believe. His role as Judge was simple. He deserved reverent fear. He could cast me into hell or allow me to come to heaven. He could speak and cause nations to crumble. Okay, I understood all that. His role as Creator was simple. Evolution was a dumb idea to me, even in school. It didn't even make common sense. Intelligent design is awesome. It was simple to relate to God on those levels. Knowing Him as Father though, presented its challenges.

It took a lot of imagination for me to figure out how to receive Almighty God as my personal, loving Daddy. I had to conjure up what I would have treated my dad like, had he been around. A bit at a time, I began to talk to God about how I felt and why I felt that way. I began to trust Him with my secrets. I began to seek His approval about things that may have been silly to other people. I began to involve Him in my daily doings and mundane tasks. I began to cry on His shoulders and expect Him to fix "it" or help me with whatever "it" was. I began to walk in the benefits of my "Dad" being King of all creation. It was so mind-blowing! I was awestruck. I could finally see that I was not *a* king's kid. I was *the* King's kid.

Though my earthly father is gone, and I will never have the physical arms of my natural father, God is more than enough for me. He has been a great Father! He has been watchful and protective over my life. He is quick to come to my rescue and He never tires of helping me in my struggles. He loves me even more than a natural father ever could. I am more than content with the Lord as my Father. He has counted me worthy to be called His daughter.

~Chapter 15~
Family Reunion 2003

One of my grandmother's sisters was truly a great woman of God. When she gave her life to the Lord, the change was spectacular and very distinctive. There was no compromise in her. She was the epitome of a sold out saint.

My great aunt was very diligent in the Word and had a passion to see souls saved. When my grandmother was sick and had only days to live, it was my great aunt that sat with her everyday and many nights. She read the Bible to her and prayed with her. God used her to get her sister, my grandmother, saved. It was because of her diligence, love, and patience that my grandmother came to know Christ as her personal Savior. A few short years later, my great aunt died herself. However, there was no sadness in the family. Everyone who knew her knew where she went. There was never a doubt in anyone's mind about the eternal state of her soul.

In July 2003, our family held its annual family reunion. At that time, I was 27 years old. I had never been to a family reunion while I was old enough to remember it. My grandmother had kept our immediate family very private. She had been hurt and rejected many times. She'd preferred to avoid a crowd of family if she could so I grew up avoiding crowds of family too. My mother was very social, but I was more like my grandmother in my personal preferences about groups of people.

At the family reunion, I realized how much I'd cheated myself out of enjoying my family. It felt so wonderful to be surrounded by familiar faces that loved me regardless of my mistakes and my past. Though I was raised a loner and was never much of a family person, having my grandmother's family together was precious to me.

Still, my family reunion was not without incident. As I happened through some of the family photos, I found a picture of my great grandfather, my grandmother's father. At first, I was thrilled to see a picture of him. He died while I was still very young. I'd held nothing but pleasant memories of him for the majority of my life. I remembered how he had never allowed anyone to spank me. In his presence, I could do no wrong. He always gave me money and I loved spending the night at his house when I was a little girl.

After I looked at his picture for a couple of minutes, though, memories began to flood back. None of them were pleasant. All of them were painful and brought on an acute panic attack inside of me. To add insult to injury, most of those memories involved others too.

There I stood in the presence of my family, looking at my cousins and wondering if they remembered too. I knew I didn't want to ask them, but every part of me wanted to know if maybe I was hallucinating. I was older than the rest by a year or more. Maybe they wouldn't remember, I reasoned within myself.

A part of me wanted someone to tell me that I was mistaken, but I knew the memory was true. I wanted always to cherish my great grandfather as a man of honor and one that loved me deeply and correctly. At the time, I felt as if the rug had been snatched from under my feet. I felt disillusioned. Still,

I had to hold it together in the midst of all those people. The tears that I couldn't cry out loud stained my very heart and soul.

My second husband, Elias, and I left the reunion to go to the store for something. While in the truck, I told him about the memory. Sometimes, I wonder if he believed me when I told him things like that. He looked bewildered. I felt bewildered. He prayed for me and told me not to mention it to anyone else. He helped me to get a grip on my mind that day. He made me realize that bringing something like that before the others would only hurt them and most likely, they wouldn't remember it either, especially since it had taken me all those years to remember it myself. He was right, so I kept my mouth shut.

As we rode home that late evening, I almost wanted to be upset with God for even allowing me to remember. I didn't see the purpose it would serve for me to remember. I didn't see why I had to be the one who always hurt and suffered through these things alone. Though I was married, my husband didn't understand that kind of stuff. He had never seen that kind of perversion in his family. Even if he had, I wouldn't have known how to receive from him.

Molestation and incest are evils perpetrated upon children to destroy them while they are young. Personally, I believe that twice as many children go through it than are reported. It has such an ugly stigma attached to it. There will always be those people who believe it was the child's fault, especially those in the family who have escaped the ravages of it, or who were never preyed upon. You will have those who try to judge the seriousness of it by the age

83

of the child. I have actually heard people say things like, *"Well, she knew better at the age of 10. That was something she wanted to do"*; or, they will say, *"If she didn't tell anyone, she wanted it to happen."* Some of them even go so far as to say things like, *"Oh, that child has been trouble all of her life. She is fast and will sleep with anybody if she slept with her own family."*

Those kinds of accusations make children *stay* quiet and take the abuse. Most children never tell. Usually, the abuse is discovered by happenstance. I think that is very sad and it says a lot about our society.

Can a 5-year-old child willfully have sex? How about a 10-year-old? Maybe a 13-year-old? Children make decisions all the time based upon their environment. No child is born knowing how to be a prostitute, for instance. She is taught how. What am I saying?

We have generations of people who have endured abuse and suffered emotional breakdowns because of it. Take, for instance, a woman who is raped and molested, and who never wants a man again. She becomes completely dysfunctional. She may even become a lesbian because she feels safer with another woman.

On the flip side, there is a woman who is raped and molested who becomes so promiscuous that any man can have her if he would simply ask. She gave up trying to keep her precious gift a long time ago. Now, she just wants to get rid of it all together. Giving it is easier than having it taken. She gives her body to protect herself from being raped, not just physically but emotionally and mentally as well.

Both sides of that coin are deadly. Both sides of the coin have to be healed and treated with delicacy. This is not the kind of pain that can be "sucked up" or covered. It must be dealt with in all diligence and love.

There was another reason I stayed quiet during our family reunion: I was very afraid of being judged. I was afraid people would look at my past and think that I chose to sleep with my great grandfather, even though I was only four or five years old. At the age of twenty-seven, it would seem that I should have known better, but my fears were grounded in my past reality. My fears had been confirmed before and I refused to go through such harsh judgment again.

Chances are that many of the people who purchase this book will have been raped or molested, or they know someone who has been. It isn't as uncommon as we would like to believe.

Molestation happens across cultural lines. It happens across racial lines. It isn't based upon intelligence. It isn't based upon financial health. It may seem to happen more in poverty-stricken communities, but I can assure you that most of it just goes unreported.

I found out the hard way that molestation isn't just a black thing or a poor thing. It is a perversion thing. It happens to God's called and chosen people, and it happens to the average Jane Doe in an average home. God created each of us with purpose. I don't believe the enemy would waste his time tempting people to molest or rape a person who has no destiny and no call upon their life. Because of the very nature of the crime, it can be nothing less than a device of the enemy, one of his strongest weapons.

Someone reading this book may think that they have never been molested when indeed they have been. A molester is a molester long before he touches his first victim. He is first guilty in his thoughts. Some men never actually touch their victims. They just think and fantasize about touching. They rent the videos of children with adults engaging in sex acts. Some molesters do it with the words of their mouths. They talk filth to children. They take advantage of their positions in those children's lives. They open a door that should not be opened by planting filthy word images in young minds. Some of you haven't actually been touched, but you have been molested.

That family reunion opened my eyes to a lot of things. Because of that repressed memory, this book exists. God had to allow a series of events to happen to make me go back and deal with my past. This testimony was freed while I was in jail.

I was arrested in August 2005 for old fines and failure to appear warrants. While I was in jail, God kept bringing the memory of what my great grandfather had done back to my mind. It seemed to torment me. It had been 2 years since I first remembered and here it was, still cropping up.

One night as I was praying, God spoke to me in a whisper and told me that I would be in jail until I learned obedience. He would never specifically tell me what I needed to do because I already knew. I was in jail for 44 days, skirting the issue, hitting and missing at what He wanted from me. Finally, I put pencil to paper and began to write. With every paragraph I was stopping and crying. It was dreadful! I didn't feel prepared for the suffering!

With every page I completed, the family reunion kept coming back up. The answer had been right before my eyes. The reason the memory continually resurfaced was that God was telling me to share my testimony with the world. He wanted to use my story to break heavy yokes of oppression, depression, worthlessness and anger off of others. In my own family, rape had happened... not only to me, but to others that I loved. I was angry. I was really angry at the devil for the first time and God helped me to channel that anger onto these pages.

My family reunion was the genesis of my assignment, my destiny. I was called to bring the light of exposure to the hidden world of familial incest and perversion inside and outside of the Church, and to bring encouragement to men and women around the world who have been victimized and disillusioned. Though this call is not easy, I wouldn't trade it for anything.

~Chapter 16~
The Stripping of Will... This is Rape

I don't believe that most people truly count the cost of their actions. Maybe some of them do, and perhaps figure in themselves that the cost is affordable for them. I will never be able to fathom the thoughts of a man or woman who can fondle and have sex with their own child, or anyone else's child for that matter. How can a person with a 5-year-old daughter sexually assault her or any other little girl or boy near the same age? It is perverse. It is a distortion of truth and consequences. It is a place where Satan lives and rules.

So many times, we as people simply jump into things. We look only at how our actions will affect our own lives. Few people are mature enough to consider how their decisions fully affect others. The result of perversity is lost innocence in our children or others who look to us for guidance and help.

I now want to delve into what this book is really about. It isn't really about me and all my issues, past and present. It isn't really about rape and molestation, though they are constants throughout my story. It is about the loss of innocence in any way.

There are two ways innocence is lost: It can either be given away, or it can be stripped away. Unfortunately, too many children and young adults are being raped of their innocence. They are over-exposed to things that tarnish their perception of life. Children are exposed to violence in the home and at school. They encounter faithless and unmerciful people, the hardest of the hard. They are ridiculed at school for being virgins in a world where virginity isn't viewed as a precious possession. Parents curse, beat, and molest children. Children follow suit with other children. Where is the voice that will stand up and declare that enough is enough?

Too many of our young people are without protection against the evil of this world. Too many of them are dying on the inside, crying out for help, but finding none – and being assimilated into a society that eventually kills them. Too many adults are treating children with disrespect and disdain. The problem is found in this key fact: Many of the adults who are trying to care for hurting children were themselves once hurting children who never found healing, acceptance, deliverance and love in their own lives.

When I was thirteen years old and before I left Little Rock, I went to what was supposed to be a teenage New Years' party with a friend and her friend who were fourteen and sixteen respectively. I was still very young and most of the people there were either grown or close to it. I found a seat beside the punch bowl and didn't move the rest of the night. I sat there and drank punch. I had no idea what *spiked* meant. I knew the punch tasted good and I was thirsty. After drinking the alcoholic (spiked) punch for two hours, I was intoxicated. Because some people there were smoking marijuana, though I would never have dared touch it myself, I got a contact high. The majority of that party is just a dusky memory. My brain is still fogged about the beginning of that night, yet, there are some things about that night I wish I could forget.

As the party drew to a close, my friends couldn't find me, and because they were looking for me, we all missed our ride. We were stuck on another side of town in the middle of the night and cell phones were not the rave back then. None of us had any money. The word stranded did little justice to how we felt.

We wandered around Little Rock, Arkansas in the wee hours of the morning looking for a way home. A few people stopped to help us, but when they found out where we lived in Little Rock, none of them would bring us home. We lived in College Station. It was considered the worst part of Little Rock for a long time. Cops had been killed there. Bad things happened there all the time, but somehow until that night, I never realized just how bad it was. No matter how big the men were, or how many people were in the vehicle when they stopped, not one person endeavored to take us even closer to home. It was horrible.

After we'd gotten ourselves trapped in an elevator in a hospital and were asked to leave, and after nearly breaking the glass doors at a closed high school while trying to get to a bathroom, someone finally stopped. The couple of men that stopped seemed nice enough. We all got into the car with them. They took us to this big white house. It was very dark and I was tired. My friend's friend pulled me aside and told me that if one of them asked, I should tell them that I was having my cycle. I wondered why she wanted me to lie. Shortly thereafter, one of the men approached us and said that for us to get home someone had to have sex with him and his friends. There were three of them and three of us. It was terrifying for me. I lied like I'd been told to do. She did the same. Everything then fell to my friend. It didn't seem to bother her to follow two of the guys back to a room. A few minutes later, I had to use the bathroom. The third guy told me where it was. As I was going, I accidentally opened the wrong door. I was devastated at what I saw. Then, another part of me was in awe and very curious. I stood there all of a minute. It seemed to me that an hour passed by. I guess I was trying to figure out what I was seeing.

After they ran me out of the room, I went back to my friend's friend. I was crying by this time. I wasn't sure what I saw, but I knew it was wrong. I was so afraid for my friend. I thought she was being hurt against her will and I felt powerless to help. My heart was breaking and those next ten minutes felt like an eternity.

When she came out of the room with those guys, I was mad at her. I'm still not sure what made me feel so angry with her. She seemed fine and we all three loaded back into the car with the two guys that she came out of the room with. They took us back to the spot we were in when they picked us up. They said they were not going to College Station or anywhere near it. I was truly angry at that point. I was fighting mad. They were very rude when they put us out of the car. Though nothing happened to me, I felt used.

After an hour or so, another two men came by and stopped for us. Each of them liked my friends. They agreed to take us home. Again, they took us to some apartments first. My friend went in with one guy as her friend and I sat in the car with the other guy. They kissed and cuddled while I sat in the back seat feeling like a disjointed thumb. It took the man and my friend a long time to come out of the house, but finally they did. I was so afraid they would trick us too, but they didn't. They actually drove us all to our very doors. I lied about where I lived because I was ashamed, but I was dropped off close enough to walk home in a couple of minutes.

That night never left my memory. We went through a lot to get home, but still made it safely in body. My mind, however, was another story. I'd learned what lies to tell to protect myself from men that would care enough to let that stop them. I'd seen a "train" in progress. God used my friend to protect me from being involved in something I wasn't ready for at my young age. Nevertheless, I had been overexposed.

There is yet another incident I would like to discuss: At the age of nine, I went to Little Rock for the summer. As summer drew to a close and we were leaving Little Rock heading to Warren, we passed by what is called The Pike. In broad daylight, there was a man on his knees before another man who was a drug dealer. It took me years to understand what I had seen. Because of my curious nature, I simply filed that incident away to ponder on later. I was flabbergasted even then, but was unsure of the reason for the nausea that suddenly hit me.

Again while in Little Rock, I was overexposed. I occasionally went to the cafes with my mother and my stepfather. I loved going because I often came home with at least twenty dollars. That was a lot of money for a nine year old child. Everyone loved to see me dance around and play music. Everyone gave me money and bought me sodas. I usually got free food too. One particular time, my grandmother came to Little Rock with me. We all went to the café. Soon as we walked in, a "woman" with long hair was dancing on the pole in the middle of the room over by the pool tables. I remember my mother calling her a "he/she". I didn't understand at first. A bit later, I figured it out. The woman wasn't a woman at all, but a man who was dressed like a woman. I was sickened. I was confused. Yet, another part of me was oddly drawn to him and I stared the whole time I was there. I alternately wanted to scream the word "yuck" at him or tell him he really looked like a woman and ask him how he did it.

As a child, I was constantly overexposed to things that I never should have seen. I saw people get stabbed. I saw a piece of a police officer's skull that had been blown out of his head a few weeks earlier. I saw my mother in the hospital with tubes running everywhere behind being shot by her husband. I heard the doctor say that she would probably die because of a bullet that was lodged inside of her. I saw domestic violence. I saw sex and things with sexual overtones everywhere I went. I was called every name you can imagine while I was still too young to be any of them.

When my son was about thirteen days old and I was fifteen, a man tried to stab my mother as she held my baby. In a rage, I attacked the man and pushed him into my grandfather's television. The knife he held poked me in my hand. The aftermath of the situation was much more than I would have preferred. Being fifteen years old, I did what any young girl would do. I told my stepfather about it. He, in turn, got a gun and went to find the man who had poked me with a knife. The tables were turned and the man almost beat my stepfather to death with his own gun. It was horrific! I wanted to fight with him, but wasn't allowed to get out of the car. I would have quickly given my life for my stepfather. I felt that somehow I was stronger than he was and that he needed me. I felt as if I had failed him. He was about to kill for me and I couldn't fight with him. It was unfair and I felt guilty about that incident for years. He was never the same after that night and a couple of years later, he died without knowing how much I loved him in spite of all that had happened. I appreciated him for what he did *for* me and I forgave him for what he did *to* me.

My innocence has been gone for a long time. I've seen more and done more than many people twice my age. Some people will read this book and think surely some of this stuff is fabricated. All of it is truth and the half won't be told in this one book.

My life was lived hard and fast. Everything was accelerated for me. At the age of eight, I was helping my grandmother pay bills. I counted all the money and separated it for whatever purposes she told me to. At the age of ten, I worked a whole GED preparation book. I even passed the geometry and algebra part. Some of it I guessed, but most of it I knew. I had my first son at the age of fifteen. I had my second son at the age of sixteen. At the age of seventeen, I moved in with my son's father. By the age of eighteen, I was officially in an abusive relationship. At age nineteen, I was married for the first time. By the age of twenty, I had stabbed someone. By the age of twenty-three, I was married for the second time, had tried to commit suicide more than three times, and had a criminal record.

My life was a mess in so many ways, but God somehow blessed me in the midst of it. Somehow, all the rape, molestation, and domestic violence that happened to me helped me learn to endure hardship. Being hated helped me learn to love people for who they are. God gave me a son when I needed him most. He spoke to me when no one in my immediate family was saved. I actually had a better prayer life before salvation than I did during my early years of knowing God. He often answered my prayers, though I wasn't saved at the time. I knew God was there and I was determined to touch Him and to live for Him at some point in my life.

I have been hit by a car twice, in 1984 and again in 1985. I could have died either time, but God spared me. Once, in 1998, I had been up for two complete days in a row with less than 20 minutes of sleep. I went out of town with a friend and my son. On the way home, I fell asleep behind the wheel. When I finally woke up, I was almost home. No one can say that I was sleep-driving and just don't remember. I was completely asleep, eyes closed and the whole nine yards. I slept for at least 25 minutes, no lie. When I woke up, it startled me! I nearly ran off the road because of how hard I jerked the wheel out of fear. All of this can be verified. I *know* there is a God and that I'm serving the right one. He loved me enough to spare my life time and time again. He showed His love for me when most people wished nothing less than death upon me.

Many people valued me less than the dirt on the ground. Many despised me. Even some of my family thought I was detestable. But, I am reminded of the scriptures found in 1 Corinthians 1:27-29:

> *But God hath chosen the foolish things of the world to confound the wise and God hath chosen the weak things of the world to confound the things which are mighty: And*

base things of the world, and things which are
despised, hath God chosen, yea, and things
which are not to bring to naught things that
are: That no flesh should glory in his presence

Though I have been despised and thought of
as nothing, it was all in God's perfect plan for my life.
I can honestly thank God now for the times when I
was weak. Because there was no able defender for me,
God gathered me to Himself. He trusted me to
endure hardships and turmoil to become more useful
to His kingdom.

Most people never mention what God truly
said to Saul before he became Paul. He told him that
He would show him what great things he *must* suffer
for His name's sake. People hate to suffer, but power
comes through suffering. Mark a person who doesn't
know how to suffer; that same person is the weakest
of the weak. It doesn't take someone special to enjoy
prosperity. Anyone can do that. However, only those
who are strong and courageous can find growth and
even joy in the midst of the deepest pits. Like Paul,
we must all suffer something for His name's sake.

Though I lost my innocence, I gained much
more in hindsight. I gained a relationship with God
and a testimony. A testimony is a powerful weapon
against the tactics of the enemy. Satan doesn't have
any new tricks. A testimony reveals him for who he
really is… a liar and the father of lies.

~Chapter 17~
When Innocence is Lost

So many times, we push abstinence and purity but do not have a healing answer for those whose purity is gone. Isaiah, the prophet, said this in chapter 50, verse 4:

> *The Lord God hath given me the tongue of the learned, that I should know how to speak a word in season to him that is weary*

Solomon puts it this way at Proverbs 25:11:

> *A word fitly spoken is like apples of gold in pictures of silver*

In my own life, I found few people who had a word of encouragement for me. Most people judged or pointed their finger. Others agreed with my issues and made excuses for me. I needed neither judgment nor sympathy, but truth. I rarely found it in those around me. I found myself often in search of an answer for my issues. The majority of the people who proclaimed to have an answer only exasperated me the more. I was a wrecked ship docked on a deserted island. I was diseased in my flesh and in my soul. There was no help. There were few to stand in the gap for me. God had to intervene.

It took a very long time for me to realize the power in the blood of our slain yet risen Savior, Jesus Christ. Somehow, I felt dirtier than even the blood of Jesus could clean. I felt out of touch and beyond the power of God. It was the blood that was shed to cover and protect me and it was the Word that was supposed to wash me. Still, it was up to God's chosen people to love me through my trial. For a very long time, I suffered from rejection both inside and outside of the church. At certain times, God would send someone to truly listen to me and care about me. For the most part, receiving love inside the church was a continuous issue for me. When I would meet people who loved me, I didn't know how to receive them. I felt suspicious because it was a very rare occasion.

For all the things that God does here on the earth, it seems He always uses a person. God rarely uses birds to bring us food as He used ravens to feed Elijah. Most people probably won't experience manna raining from heaven in their lifetime. God uses us to minister to each other, and it is shameful for the Body of Christ not to have an answer for those who are hurting. Where can a person find the answer if not in the Church? If a person cannot trust the people in today's churches to really love them, where should they search for love?

Everyday the Kingdom of God is losing people to the streets. Children are searching for answers to their troubles. If the Church does not have the answer for these children, the streets will pacify them with a lie.

Everyday, neglected and unloved women take up the search for an answer to their pain. They search for unconditional love. The local assemblies of the saints proclaim to have the answer, yet their profession isn't backed with action. Hurting people come to church day after day and leave the same way they came. Some people come into the churches heavy hearted and burdened. They then leave disillusioned and hopeless.

Though this may not be the case everywhere, unfortunately, it is the case for a lot of people. Therefore, I lend you this advice: If you are blessed with great leadership in your home church, stay there even when you don't understand everything. The grass is probably not greener on the other side of the fence.

One of the things we don't seem to understand is that not everyone is able to endure the heartache of unfaithful and unloving Christians. For centuries, the church, as an institution, has been lifted up as a beacon of light for the hopeless, the destitute and the mournful. When people come and find it to be anything short of a loving assembly, not all of them will recover. In that case, who is guilty? We can't blame it on the devil, but must cleanse our own hearts from hypocrisy. It's okay to have a bad day or moment in life. It's a different thing to habitually practice behaviors that cause the morale of in the Church to decline.

When innocence is lost, the Body of Christ should be positioned to take in the hurting souls. It is our job to nurture people and give them back to God.

Many children have lost faith in adults. Some children are not raised with parents that understand what it is to protect their children. Some children need protection from the very people that *should* protect them. Some children are defenseless against the adults in their lives.

In my childhood, my problems were not with other children. My problems came from adults forcing me to grow up too fast. My problems came from men who refused to allow me a childhood. My problems came about when the people who were supposed to protect me did not do what they promised. I'm only one person. There are many more who have endured similar or worse problems.

When innocence is lost too early, a young person's world can soon deteriorate into a pit of darkness. When life seems continually dark from a very young age, hope is easily lost. As adults, we should seek to protect children, even if the children are not our own. We should foster a child's individuality while yet cultivating the attributes of Christ in them. We should provide a safe haven for children, giving them a place where they can grow into who God called them to be without fear of harm or negativity. We all have a part to play in protecting and safeguarding children since they cannot do it for themselves.

Of course, not only children are affected by the darkness in this world. Adults are just as often disheartened by the cruelty in the world as children are. For those blessed to go through life in a somewhat naïve state, the sure awakening to the brutality of life can be very disturbing. Life doesn't just happen to the unsaved, but life happens even to the saved. Life happens inside and outside of churches. Life happens to people of all ages and in all cultures. To live means to endure hardships and trials. Adults are sometimes robbed of their ability to bear up under burdens. Just like children, many adults are forced to realize that not everybody in their lives mean them well.

In my own life, many times I was dismayed at how fickle friends can be, at how phony saints can be and at how easily hurt I could be. It seemed that just as I figured myself out, a change would come. Just when I thought I couldn't cry any longer, more tears would make their way to my eyes. I found myself distraught in the world and disenchanted in the fellowship of believers. I wondered where my answer would come from. I had no role models and nothing tangible that I could grab hold of. I felt destined for history to repeat itself.

I was an honor roll student. Of course, my mom had been an honor student too. She was probably a shoe-in for valedictorian, but she quit school. She had too much happening in her life. She had a baby at the young age of fifteen and then I came along at the age of eighteen. I myself had closely followed in her shoes. I had two sons very close together and while quite young. Eventually, I quit school in the eleventh grade. My mom went on in her later years to get her GED; I too, went right on to a vocational school and received my GED. Though my mom never went to college, God blessed me with a scholarship still and the opportunity to go to school with all expenses paid. I struggled to complete two semesters of college. I was tired already with even the thought of living. I had been through the wringer in relationships and with bad decisions. I was still suffering from the lack of a balanced childhood. Because I never responded well to discipline as a child, in my adult years I quickly learned to remove myself from any situation that became too difficult for me. Because I hadn't enjoyed a full childhood, as an adult I experienced childish relapses, attempting to regain what was stolen from me. Once the blinders of innocence are ripped away, there is no putting them on again. To try to replace them does an injustice to the person who lost their innocence. To ignore the problem makes the problem worse.

There is a terrible injustice both in the world and in today's churches, a common ground, if you will. Neither the world nor some churches like to be confronted with issues of moral decay and degradation. People hate to come face to face with any issue that shows they have been failing in their duties. It is not customary for most people to deal honestly with themselves. It's easier to deal with others from far off distances. A child marrying her teacher in another state is considered "sad and heart-wrenching", but we only shake our heads at it. It's news and nothing more. It serves as entertainment, in crudest sense of the word. Of course, if *our* child marries his/her teacher, then it becomes an outrage and something must be done! How sad! Innocence is innocence, whether far off or close to home.

When innocence is lost and even beforehand, the answer is always found in Christ Jesus. No matter the circumstance or trial, we must learn to develop a relationship with God, and to introduce our children to God while helping them to build a relationship with Him for themselves.

~Chapter 18~
Deception

While reading this book, I hope that none of you presumes to think this book is singularly about rape and molestation. This book is about a great deal more than that. It is about the deceptions we encounter when we make a game of life. Just as I came to a place where I was lulled into believing I was safe, so too do most people. All people go through times when Satan tries to deceive us, though I've come to recognize the tactics of the enemy.

In 2004, at the age of twenty-eight years old and while a minister, I was raped by another minister. Before that humbling event, I thought that surely as an adult, I could defend myself. I figured, I was stronger, not just in my body but also in my mind. I believed in myself to keep myself safe. Satan had tricked my mind into believing that protection from harm could be found in my own strength. Because I never trusted anyone fully, I learned from a young age to rely only on myself. Though my grandmother had raised me for the majority of my life, even she did not have my full trust. However, on that awful night in 2004, I came face to face with the reality of my own weaknesses and inabilities. On that night, God allowed me to see that unless my trust was in Him, anything could happen.

I still remember that night as if it were yesterday. I had been living in Arkansas for a brief period. My church home in Louisiana was having a conference and I was there to support the prophet I'd recommended as speaker that night. At the end of the night, some of us gathered together and took the prophet out to eat. During conversation, as we were waiting for our food, an insulting remark was made by a minister that hurt my feelings. It was probably just a joke and not meant to hurt, but it did nonetheless. My skin wasn't as thick as it must've seemed at that time. At that point, I shut down. (The spirit of offense will set you up every time.) Nothing else would be heard from me that night. Still, I believe the prophet picked up on how alienated the minister's comment made me feel. Of course, at that point, it wasn't hard for me to feel alienated because I had been hurt repeatedly by these same people in my church home. Nevertheless, I held my peace and went on. I didn't want anyone to know that my feelings were truly hurt from the laughter at something I didn't deem funny at all.

Because I had taken that comment so hard, I determined in myself I would just sleep in my car that night. I lied to my pastor about where I was going. I lied to everyone around me because I didn't want them to know how torn up I was. As I was leaving my pastor's house, my phone rang. It was the prophet. He told me that God had shown him that I intended to sleep in my car and that I had been hurt by the comment that evening. He asked that I come to his room because he wanted to talk to me and pray with me. I never thought about whether he was trustworthy. I guess I assumed that he was. I figured that he was a prophet and people who were anointed like that had to be living right. I had driven him from Arkansas to Louisiana. He knew my pastor in Arkansas, and had just preached a word for my pastor in Louisiana. He had a gift and knew the truth about the intents of my heart. Why would I doubt him? I went to hear what he had to say to me. It was already midnight. I was truly scared to follow through with my plans, so I figured he would be a good way to stay awake a little longer before going to the park or the Wal-mart parking lot to get a little sleep.

When I got there, he talked to and prayed for me. He offered some good counsel to me. He told me that allowing myself to be so easily offended made me vulnerable. He said all the right things. Somehow, I trusted him a little bit. Maybe in truth, I trusted his gifted, not yet realizing that gifts come without repentance, though I preached it. (It's funny how we can preach something and still not *know* it.) He finally offered me his bed and said he would be more than happy to sleep on the couch in the room. At first, I was a bit skeptical. It didn't take a lot of convincing for me though. I believed in his integrity, mostly because of the gift he had. I had seen him in action in the ministry a time or two before that night and I thought that he was a hard-hitting, bold, in-your-face kind of prophet. So, as much as I hate to admit it, I did trust him because I was still much more naïve than I want to confess. I decided I would stay there with him. He laid down on the couch and I laid in the bed, on top of the covers with all my clothes and my shoes still on. I didn't trust him enough to let my guard completely down. I don't know what I thought shoes would do.

In the beginning, my mind was still full of what happened and what I should have said to my own defense, so sleep came slowly. Finally, I did go to sleep and obviously, a deep slumber came upon me. I remember trying to turn over from my back. I felt stuck or something. I couldn't breathe very well. All the lights were off in the room when I opened my eyes. When I fell asleep, the lamp had been on. I was disoriented and sleepy. It took me at least a full minute to realize a man was on top of me and that

105

was why I couldn't move. Then I began to plead with him as he was scratching me up with his toenails trying to get my stockings down. I was weak and tired from all the staying up and moving around that week. At that time, I had no idea that it was Grave's Disease which was actually taking such a physical toll on me like that. All I knew then was that I had weak spells and heart palpitations. It was still undiagnosed and untreated. Sometimes, I imagine that I could have fought him off better if I hadn't been half dead without knowing it. Nevertheless, I tried everything I could, but my stockings and clothes were working against me and when I started trying to resist, he put my arms under his knees. I finally relented in hopes of it ending soon. I stopped fighting but I kept talking about God to him, telling him that God wouldn't be pleased and that he was supposed to be a man of God and finally, it was over. It probably only lasted two to four minutes, but it felt like an eternity.

Afterwards, he sat on the edge of the bed feeling guilty. I laid there feeling powerless and dirty. I felt like a child again. To me, I was still an eleven-year-old girl who needed someone to care about and protect her. He apologized to me. I barely heard him through the multitude of thoughts that were plaguing my mind. After awhile, though I have no idea how long, I got up and got in my car. It was still dark. It had to have been before 2:00 in the morning. I was determined to make it back home to Texarkana and to safety. Still, another part of me wanted my mother. The child in me wanted to go home and tell her mother. The adult knew that would do very little good.

I don't think I drove fast. Somehow, the road just seemed to disappear behind all the thoughts. I didn't cry or scream. I just pondered everything in my mind and wondered if I should even talk to God about it at all. I knew that He knew already, and some part of me wondered why He'd allowed that to happen to me again. I had to sift through my feelings. I wasn't even sure it was rape. I had never been sure if the rapes were rapes. Because it was my tendency, if I couldn't get away, to zone out, I always felt at least partially responsible. I also couldn't shake the feeling that he'd accosted me because I had shared my past with him. He *knew*. I guess he figured my past justified his actions. I drove the long way around to get home. Finally, I pulled up in front of my apartment in Texarkana around 5:30 in the morning. It was still dark. I wasn't tired, but I was still afraid. I knew when I walked in the house that my fiancé would know something had happened to me. I wasn't sure he would believe me if I told him, and I wasn't sure I would tell him.

As soon as I walked in the room, I laid my head on him. He woke up and immediately asked what was wrong. At that point, all the tears came. They weren't just tears for that moment, but tears for every moment that happened to me. Before that morning, I had never truly grieved for all that had befallen me throughout my life. At that point, I knew I trusted him and I knew he loved me. He sat up and held me. Then he asked me what the prophet had done to me. He knew somehow. He knew without me actually saying anything. I loved him for that. I appreciated him for that. I told the story in sobs and tears, and we called Pastor Bradford, my temporary shepherd. He was already up and already on his way to my house.

When Pastor Bradford pulled up, I felt somehow angry at him. I don't know why I felt so suspicious of him, but I did. He talked to me about it and then he tried to call the man who had violated me, his prophet friend whom I'd recommended to speak at the engagement in Louisiana. Near the end of the conversation, he said something that angered and frustrated me. He said, concerning the prophet, "One day, you will thank him for it."

Surely, Pastor Bradford was right. I can now thank that man for many things. I can thank him for helping me to see my own frailty. Because of him, I learned that God alone is my stay. God is my fortress and my strong tower. In God, I can trust. I thank him for showing me that not all people with spiritual gifts are godly. I thank him for helping me to realize how sex turns to perversion so easily. I thank him for helping me to realize I was not yet healed from my past. I especially thank him for showing me that his sin was no greater than my own sin. When the prophet apologized to me, I accepted it with my words, though it was more than a year later when God helped me to forgive him. However, I did accept my own vulnerability. It was because I lacked temperance and was easily offended that I even went to his room. *That* part was my fault. He taught me to guard my vulnerability. He taught me to guard my pains. Not everyone can be trusted with them.

After I finished talking with Pastor Bradford, I went back in the house and laid down beside Mike. I don't know why exactly, but I do know that night changed our relationship forever. I had been searching for someone who made me feel safe my entire life. He made me feel safe. He just held me (and he promised to kill him for me, which was very

108

comforting for me to hear at that time). Of course, he didn't kill him, but his threat served its purpose in my life that night. He told me he would never let anything happen to me. To the best of his ability, he tried to keep his promise. He tried to protect me, sometimes even from some things that I needed to endure. That night, he was a shoulder to cry on and an encouraging minister to me. Though we were living in sin because we were living together outside of marriage, for the first time I felt as if I knew whom I was destined to marry and love for the rest of my life. I felt complete and whole with him. He was God's tangible person in my life that could exemplify God's loving attributes to me.

I would like to tell you that my story only got better from there, but that would be a lie. Satan continued to fight me. He continued to try to seduce with me lies. I continued to wrestle with self-condemnation. Even today, some of the issues that were born in me when I was still a child haunt me. Sometimes, I have to check my motives and my heart for signs of the remnants of pain from my childhood. At times, I find myself looking at men and thinking terrible thoughts, simply because they compliment me or because they stare just a moment too long, and especially if they are sporting a wedding band. Sometimes, I actually ask God what He was thinking to make a man and then give Him headship. Of course, I already know the answer to that question. In all actuality, women would make a bigger mess of things. Men were created for headship, but not all of them have been taught how to be who God created them to be.

I know in my knower that not all men are bad. In fact, many men are good, as much as any person can be. My husband proves it to me everyday. This book is about wrong actions, which can be perpetrated by man or woman. I can't say that the general state of manhood isn't in jeopardy, but so is the state of womanhood as God had originally intended and still desires. There is nothing more beautiful than a man who can stand his ground and be sold out to God. The same goes for a woman. Yet, there is nothing worse than a man who won't be what he was created to be. I will never change my feelings in this one area: if men won't stand up and be the leaders this world needs, then we all are in trouble. As a woman, I can only tell my story. I can only speak from my own experiences and convey what I have learned through them.

Another one of my thoughts on this subject is that as long as women try to play the role of a man, things will continually be out of order. God gave men headship. Men were created for the job. God gave woman the position of support. Women were created for that job. When a support structure is placed in the position of headship, things go berserk quickly. Support structures cannot handle the extra pressure of headship. When headship is placed in a position to only support, both parties will be miserable.

There are many deceptions in the world and in our churches today. There is the deception of offense, the deception of fear, the deception of manipulation, the deception of authority and so forth.

The deception of offense is a dangerous deception. One of the reasons there are churches on every corner in some cities is because of the deception of offense. Someone was hurt and offended by someone else and decided they could do better on their own. Someone might have told them they should become a pastor. Offense does make us vulnerable. It shuts down our ability to reason. We begin to think through emotions rather than truth. Offense is the deception that has hurt me the most. Many times when I was hurt or in a bad predicament as an adult stemmed from me being offended by something someone said or did. The deception of offense is centered in pride.

No matter what area the enemy is trying to bring deception in, only truth can break it. Truth is found in the Word of God. Deception uses facts, but truth overpowers fact. Deception always comes from self-centeredness and pride, but if we would humble ourselves, we could gain victory in many areas in our lives. We have to choose neither to be deceived nor to deceive anyone else. The most potent of any deception is self-deception. When we practice denial, we make truth our enemy. No one yields to an enemy; our natural instinct is to fight against an enemy.

There were times in my life when I practiced deception and thought of the truth as an enemy. The very few friends I had watched me become alienated because I refused to hear what God was saying to me. In my fight to maintain the life I had built on lies, I pushed God's truth away from me. In that place, I thought I would surely perish, that all hope was lost!

I encourage every reader to accept *the* Truth as *the* guide in this life. We only get one chance to get life right, and to enjoy that abundant life Christ came to give us. If we allow ourselves to live in lies, deception and denial, we murder our chances at having that Christ-like life promised us in the Bible.

~Chapter 19~
The Residue of Pain

In the churches I attended, I encounter one thing more than anything else: people who were still full of the residue of their past. These people often come to church faithfully. They are quick to get in the prayer lines. They praise God and have a consistent prayer life. Nevertheless, they somehow cannot seem to get free from the residue of their pain. It comes out when someone gets close to them. It shows itself in anger, backbiting, jealousy and envy.

The residue is the stuff left behind after a cleaning. Have you ever cleaned a toilet and it looked sparkling white to the human eye? I can assure you that you still would not drink out of it. Why wouldn't you? Because you know it may appear clean, yet it's still a toilet and anything could be lurking there. Even when we take baths or showers, it seems no matter how long the bath and how hot the water, we can never get clean enough.

When we have lived for any length of time and gone through any storm that bought pain to us, we find that the residue can live long after the thing that caused the pain has been removed. For some people, they don't understand why they get angry so quickly about some things and not about other things. Some people don't know why certain smells and certain music can throw them into a tizzy. Some people truly don't understand why they begin to feel depressed when certain things are said about them. They seek an answer for their issues, but find none. They want to be free from their pasts yet find themselves bound to the old person they were and what happened yesterday. Some people suffer the

112

majority of their lives over something that lasted only a few months many years before.

I grew up in a very unfavorable environment. I suffered through many different kinds of pain. Still, all of that was in my past. How is it that I can still cry over what happened to me twenty-two years ago? Why do pictures bring back the acute sensations of pain at certain times but not at others? Why do I still feel the need to make people in my life prove their love for me? This is the residue of what once had been.

No one is raping or molesting me now. No one is beating me. No one is currently lying on me to my knowledge. I am an adult now. Though my relationship with my mother *was* damaged, she is yet alive for me to speak to whenever I desire to speak to her. Actually, no one is rubbing my face in my mistakes or saying I won't make it anymore. No one who has ever done or said these things to me lives in my home or sees me everyday. Yet, sometimes it feels like only yesterday when someone was doing all those things to me. It is not the actions that hurt me anymore. It is the residue of the actions. It is because I remember them that I hurt. It is because it hurts to remember the actions that I respond in ways unbecoming at times. I may not always know what motivates some of my actions or words. Sometimes, a wound will close on the outside, so that you no longer think about it, but on the inside is infection and rottenness. This is the state of much of the world today in one aspect or another. Some childhood pain causes a young girl to be "easy". Some rejection by a young girl in elementary school causes a guy to grow up disliking brunettes. I mean, the list can be endless.

113

Sometimes, the people of God refuse to validate how powerful a memory can be. In the churches today, we've grown accustomed to wanting things to appear a certain way. We teach the people how to *act* healed and delivered. We no longer tarry, cry and pray with the people to ensure they *are* healed and delivered. We tell them the lie that they need to just suck it up and move on. We tell them that the past is just good for testimony. We leave them in bondage to the memories because we don't want to deal with hurting people. We don't feel as if we have the time to help someone grieve for what was stolen from them or for what they gave away that was precious to them. We've been erroneously taught that time matters more than people. Some ministers have bought into the great lie of the enemy. We believe we do people a justice if we teach them how to grieve silently. We believe we do people a justice if we teach them how to act whole. Still, a broken person can never act whole. No amount of faking fools God, and rarely can we fool ourselves for very long. The truth eventually comes out.

What defenses are there against the residue? There are only three defenses, all of them working together. We must forgive, love more abundantly and share our pains with others. Before we can truly love those that spitefully misuse us, we have to forgive them. Once we've forgiven, love isn't an unreasonable request. In fact, it is the next logical step for a believer of Jesus Christ. The only thing left after love is to share our testimony. When healing comes, our testimony is easy to release. We release it, not with malice or ulterior motives, but we release it in hopes of God being able to spare or heal someone from the pain and pressure we've been through.

~Chapter 20~
I Know She Didn't Say FORGIVE?

An old adage says, "Forgiveness is golden". What the adage doesn't tell us is that forgiveness is not always easy. Forgiveness does not always happen quickly. Sometimes, forgiveness forces us to look at ourselves.

Forgiveness is not forgetting. Those are two separate incidences. Forgiveness is allowing an otherwise guilty person to enjoy the benefits of someone that is innocent. Forgiveness is to pardon a person of their wrongdoings, not desiring to see retribution upon them. Does this make the art of forgiving more difficult? You bet. Does this mean forgiving is impossible? No, it does not.

Though most of us can't erase our memory with amnesia, selective or otherwise, we *can* forgive. We do not have to forget what was done to forgive it. We just have to make a decision to let go of what was done to us. The tricky part is when we forgive, we make a vow to the person we are forgiving that we will never bring up the offense again unless it's for a testimony. When people tell us to forget, they are actually telling us to drop it.

Another aspect of forgiveness is to realize that no one is innocent. Have you ever despised some sin or another? Have you found yourself hating a thief? If so, have you ever lied or embellished the amounts on your taxes to get more money or pay less into the government? Have you ever found yourself hating a liar? Have you ever lied to protect someone or yourself? Sometimes, while we so harshly judge each other, we find that we are guilty ourselves of the same things. We hate it when someone lies to us, yet we ourselves lie to others. We can't stand to be belittled for anything, yet we belittle others. We hate it when people gossip about us, but in our effort to defend ourselves, we do the same thing to them and to others. Forgiveness isn't hard when we realize how much we have hurt others. We all need forgiveness for something. We obtain forgiveness by giving forgiveness. We obtain mercy by giving mercy. In the same way we don't always deserve either one, we should give unmerited forgiveness and mercy.

In the many times my heart was broken, my body was used, I was lied to or lied about, and forgiveness was not something I mastered or appreciated. Rather, I became vengeful. I became a person who held grudges for years. Though most of the grudges were not visible, they were real, nonetheless. To some degree, I could have described myself as an opportunist. I knew the time would surely come when the person who hurt me would need me. The problem with that is many times my heart wouldn't allow me to turn people away. Sometimes, I found myself stuck between two opinions. I couldn't forgive and I couldn't punish.

The Bible tells us if we don't forgive, we won't be forgiven. I read that scripture many times in my early years of salvation, but it only tripped me up. I began to say I forgive with my mouth, but my heart told me a different story. I would fool myself into thinking I had forgiven someone, but I had only suppressed my anger. To me, out of sight was out of mind. Some things I thought I was past, but when put in the wrong situation, anger would rear its ugly head every time. During that time, I had to discover the

116

beauty of mercy. I had to learn mercy's role in forgiveness.

To forgive is to have mercy upon the trespasses of the person who hurt you. Sometimes, it seems a tall order to forgive. When people take something important from you, it can be hard to forgive. For me to forgive the rapes was difficult. For me to forgive the molestation was hard. For me to forgive what I deemed abandonment was excruciating.

It seems the deeper the pain, the harder the process. Yet, we are not to be so shallow that we deal only with the surface of an issue. We must go deeper to understand why forgiving is sometimes the hardest thing a person ever has to do. For many of us, giving of our time or our money is not a big deal. Some of us have even learned to appreciate other people to a point of sincere gratitude for any kindness paid to us. Yet, there are those of us that lack the one thing. That one thing is mercy.

Mercy activates compassion and understanding. Mercy knows that no one is perfect. All have come short of the glory of God. Mercy knows that even the victim has been the perpetrator at some point in time. Mercy knows none is innocent. Because none is innocent, we must be quick to have mercy upon those who hurt us. Truly, we must realize we have wronged someone before. At some point in our lives, we have inflicted unnecessary pain upon someone else. We have all done some things that we need mercy for right now, if not from people, from God. The Bible tells us if we are merciful, we will obtain mercy.

Mercy comes through love. This love is not the kind of love we are used to professing. This is not an evaporating, capricious, conditional love. Mercy comes from agape love. Some people call agape the God kind of love. This love isn't segregated only to God, but it incorporates how we should love God and people too. I don't want to make this book into a book of theology, but it's only fair to give forgiveness a thorough explanation. It is through love and mercy that forgiveness is made a manifested reality. Forgiveness is our only way to true and complete healing and deliverance.

As we endeavor on our Christian journey, we will often find ourselves being pulled and swayed by the forces of life. No one will live in this world, whether saved or unsaved, and escape turmoil, conflict and hurts. Each person will endure the full measure of what they are able to handle. Some theologians may get upset with me for the previous statement, but the truth sets us free.

Let me make another controversial statement. Because God is sovereign, He is in control and acutely aware of all things, past, present and future. Regardless of how awful your past may seem, God knew you could handle it. He trusted you to endure it and come out with a sound mind and the testimony of victory. God sometimes does more than allow things to happen. He wills them so. Am I saying that every terrible thing in your life happened because God willed or desired it? No! What I am saying is that every terrible thing that happened in your life had purpose behind it and that God knew about it long before it happened. Many preachers and Bible scholars tell us that God has a perfect will and a permissive will. I don't agree with that statement at all. God is perfect and everything about Him is perfect. His will, one will, is perfect. To this day, I've never seen anything that backs the perfect/permissive will claim, though I have seen God show mercy. Some people use Job's suffering as proof that God simply allows some things. None of them are looking closely enough. Read Job chapter 1. God used Satan. He put Satan onto Job. Satan didn't come up with Job's name. God called attention to him; the Father knew what Job would do and what he could handle. What am I saying? And, what does all that have to do with forgiveness?

Sometimes, we find it hard to forgive because the wrongs, in our mind, ruined our lives. We feel like we would be further along if we hadn't gone through certain things. We blame people for being a hindrance and a burden. We blame their acts on their own evil hearts. Still, that is not always the case. I am a firm believer in God being sovereign. He knew all of what would happen in my life before one of my days ever came to be. He willed to work all of it for my growth, for my good, and for His glory. He is God of all things, all people, all places, all times and all actions. He is in control at all times of all things going on in the heavens and in the earth. Though the actions of people may hurt us, we must look beyond the natural to understand what God is really doing. The reason some of us are always going through such strenuous times is to draw us away from the cares of the world. It is only when we become consumed with living life that we make ourselves prone to pain. God, in His infinite mercy and love, permits the winds of adversity to blow through our lives so that we can grow and mature in Him.

At times because of the greatness of God's purpose in our lives, God has to lift His hand a bit higher from our lives so that some things may happen that otherwise would not. God may permit a rape, a bad marriage, an abusive husband, a cheating wife, an alcoholic parent, a drug addict sister, a disobedient child or sickness to plague your life for a season. Most of the things that come are done at the hands of a person. If we are stuck in a natural way of thinking, we will never forgive people to the fullest measure God requires. We must realize that God knows best for our lives. Our crosses are specifically designed for us. God is just and never gives us more than we are able to overcome with Him. He wants our flesh overwhelmed so that we will desire to come to Him, the Rock who is higher, stronger, wiser and more loving than we are. He is an abundant help. When we have God, we have more than enough to get through any trial and turn it around to a victory.

Now, here I want to clarify one more thing. I don't believe God wants anyone raped, molested or abused in any fashion. Nonetheless, we live in a sinful world where sinful things happen, but we serve a God who has already seen the end and has already worked our mistakes and misfortunes into His PERFECT will for our lives! (Hopefully, that keeps people from labeling me an apostate. LOL!)

Forgiveness causes us to ask ourselves hard questions. In my quest to forgive those in my past, I had to ask myself some questions that made me face reality. One thing that God revealed to me was my guilt. As God played the movie of my life through my mind, I saw things from His perspective. No one has a right to hold a grudge. Everyone has wronged someone. Everyone has caused someone some pain.

None of our hands are clean in the matter of offense. Not all of us have *tried* to hurt someone else, yet we all have done just that. If by chance someone could say they have never offended or hurt someone else, all of us have offended God with our lifestyles. All of us have come short of God's laws.

Some people suffer large amounts of pain and turmoil. We must be able to forgive some things the world will tell us has caused irreparable damage. Still, God knows the power of an act is multiplied when we do not forgive the person and their act. Forgiveness isn't even about the person who committed the offense. Forgiveness is for us. Why should you continue to suffer from your past well into your future? Why should you lend the act of violation against you more power than it already has? Why should you destroy yourself with stress, anger and unforgiveness?

When someone lies about you, steals from you, molests you, rapes you or abandons you, they indeed hurt you. Nevertheless, when you spend your time brewing over it, you are now hurting yourself. When you hold too closely to the memories of your past, you allow every past hurt to cause more future hurt.

You can always tell when you have not forgiven. Each time someone does something or says something that seems a bit too much like what happened yesterday, the reaction from you is rash. You have allowed that one thing to link up with everything from your past. You then end up with one large mass, rather than a pimple. Somehow, everything reminds you of everything else, and so the story goes with you collecting hurts, slights and bitterness. Then, you find that it becomes harder and harder to move on with life. You find yourself feeling stuck. When you refuse to forgive, the infection of bitterness will affect your whole self. Truly, it will eat away at your marriage, your children, your job and your mental stability. All in all, it will destroy your relationship with God. He simply tells us that if we don't forgive, we will not be forgiven.

Forgiveness brings healing to you. When you allow yourself to forgive, you allow yourself to heal and be free from the wrongs of yesteryear. If you practice forgiveness, not everything will amass with something else. Each new incident in life will simply be a bump in the road of life, yet it will be powerless to stop you.

If you cannot find it in yourself to forgive for the sake of freeing yourself, forgive for the sake of everyone else who is attached to you. Bitterness causes more suffering. Now stop right here......... inhale deeply......... now exhale.

Have you not yet suffered enough?!!!

~Chapter 21~
To Rebuild the Temple

When tragedy strikes, you must replenish the areas of your losses. Weathering a storm is indeed difficult. Still, it takes nothing short of a miracle to replace and restore the things lost in the midst of a storm. It takes dedication and hard work to build and redefine your life after a storm. You must re-train your mind to think in terms of God having the final voice in your life.

For me, rebuilding came at a very high cost. There were people and things I had to loose in order to gain the fullest measure of healing God had for me. I had to walk away from some relationships that I deemed very important. I had to suffer through points of natural destitution. I had to pray my way through the temptation to turn back with every attack of the enemy. I had to praise my way through a broken home, a broken heart and depression. I had to turn away from the easier paths and face ridicule and rejection for following what I knew God was speaking to me. I cried many days because the weight of change was heavy upon me.

For me, before the rebuilding process began, I had to make some hard choices. I had to face some fears that ate at me night and day. I had to release myself to the hands of God, trusting that He knew best. The words of Job's mouth many centuries ago rang true in my own life. Though I knew God was slaying me, I still had to trust Him. I felt as if I was before a firing range. I felt mutilated. I felt uncovered and naked before a cruel world. I felt humiliated by my Father who I thought would always cover me. Yet, the firing range was not people. It was the Word of God. The mutilation was of my flesh and not of my spirit. The nakedness was before the eyes of my King and not of my sisters and brothers in Christ. He never humiliated me. He only humbled me so that His glory would be evident.

What does the term, rebuild, mean? It means to restructure, reconstruct, restore, recreate, remodel or re-establish. It was the latter of those words that God opened for my understanding to be enlightened.

The very purpose of a storm is to destroy, degrade or disassemble. So then, when a storm presents itself in our lives, we quickly assume that destruction is inevitable and permanent. We get depressed and despondent. However, without storms, there is no opportunity to build, renew and replenish those virtues in our lives that hold us together.

Sometimes, we are unwilling to obey God and purge our lives. In His great love for us, He purges our lives for us. He sends a storm, knowing in the aftermath, a great opportunity to prosper and grow will be all that is left. I am reminded of the prophet Isaiah's writings in chapter 6, verse 1:

> *In the year that king Uzziah died I saw also the Lord sitting upon the throne, high and lifted up, and his train filled the temple.*

Some things we will never see while certain entities occupy our lives. Some revelations we will never get. Some blessings are withheld. There is some power we will never walk in as long as king Uzziah is in the way.

In my life, my grandmother was my first king Uzziah. She was my lifeline. I could always depend on her and because I could, I never endured anything. I ran to her in my tight spots. She died in 1998. My second king Uzziah was my second husband, Elias. He was always there to bail me out of all my troubles. He gave all he had and with everything in him, he never allowed me to want for much of anything money could buy. We separated in 2004 and eventually divorced.

My third king Uzziah was sex. By far, this king was truly a reigning king. I turned to sex when I was happy. I turned to sex when I was sad. Sex cheered me up. Sex helped all my frustrations. Sex was more than a king... it was a god in my life. Through many trials and much suffering, God allowed heartache to minister to me. The total fulfillment of this deliverance came when I became Mrs. Lensey C. Hayes on April 28, 2007.

Sometimes, we misjudge the implications of strongholds. We underestimate the power of releasing our stays. Only when we release our worldly stays can God become our supernatural stay. When God becomes our stay, the rebuilding process can begin.

Before we can erect anything, the foundation must be sure. Building on a foundation that is unstable is a detriment to the edifice you are constructing. Our foundation must be Jesus Christ. Everything else we build on is sinking sand. No other foundation can support what we are building. No other foundation can support the temple of God.

It takes Jesus to mend all the ripped, ragged and torn edges and pieces of our lives. It takes Jesus to bring some form of a method to all the madness in our lives. It takes Jesus to guide us to peace and clarity when we are in the midst of confusion, doubt and self-pity. He is the foundation that is sure.

Through faith and obedience, we must learn to yield and allow God to work in our lives. It is through trust and relationship with God that He is able to construct the most beautiful of all things... a yielded vessel, prepared and ready for every good work. There is nothing more beautiful than a saint who has been through the wringer yet is still standing by faith, ready to obey God at the first sound of His voice. There is nothing more beautiful, to me, than a person who praises God through disconnected utilities, sick bodies, deaths in the family and lack of money. When I walk into a church with genuinely happy people, I they maintain their joy by choice because no one's life is perfect. Yet, they've been built by the very hand of God to show forth His praises. They've learned to suffer without losing their joy, their praise or their love.

I believe suffering prepares us to walk away from the world. It is only when the world has hurt and betrayed us that some of us will fully desire God, as unfortunate as that may be. I'm reminded of how my son loved bananas as a child. My grandpa used to buy him bananas every few days. He just couldn't get enough. Then one day, out of the blue, everything changed and bananas began to make him sick. It took nearly three or four years for him to begin eating them again. In those years, by default, grapes became the next going thing with my son. That's how many of us accept God: by default.

I've learned that though a person can teach us *how* to love God, no one can teach us *to* love Him. We can be taught how to pray, though no one can make us pray. It is through trials and tribulation, through pain and agony, through pressure and frustrations that we learn to love God for who He is. We learn to obey Him when we realize His decrees are for our own good. We learn to appreciate Him when we come face to face with what is killing us. It isn't a relationship with God that makes our lives hard. It is the lack thereof.

Nothing worth constructing can be built without God. No matter what comes into our lives, it is through God that we are able to recover and grow. The storms of our lives should be used as a point of reference, as a testimony and as an instructor. Storms should not halt or hinder our growth, faith or trust in God. And most definitely, they should not affect our love walk towards God or others. To the contrary, storms should build us, causing us to trust God more and to have greater faith in Him. Through storms and trials, turmoil and pain, our faith has the potential to grow exponentially!

To rebuild your temple, put all your faith in God. Leave the pain of your past behind you, bringing only the testimony of your healing and deliverance from it to the future so that someone else can be set free.

To rebuild your temple, give God your pain and realize He was there all the time.

~Chapter 22~
In The Aftermath

After going through molestation and then rape, and after surviving depression and failed suicide attempts, and after living through not one but two divorces, and after losing a child and my ability to conceive naturally, and after nearly losing my freedom, and nearly my life due to illness, I came to the knowledge that it was all for my making.

I remember a scripture that used to trouble me. I could never figure out why Jesus would pray the way He chose to pray. He told Peter at Luke 22:31-32:

> *"...Simon, Simon, behold, Satan hath desired to have you, that he may sift you as wheat: But I have prayed for thee, that thy faith fail not: and when thou art converted, strengthen thy brethren."*

Jesus never prayed for Simon Peter's deliverance from the sifting process. He didn't seem to mind a whole lot that the sifting would occur. Jesus' only concern seemed to stem from Peter's faith. A person could rightfully assume that Jesus was all for the sifting.

I can imagine Peter's face when Jesus dropped that revelation on him. I can imagine that he wondered about it, especially the sifting part. I'm sure that he, like us, had no idea the pain, the humiliation, the helplessness, or the turmoil that accompanies sifting. But we, just like him, must endure the sifting process. We must be prepared to go through the sifter to become what God intended for us to be all along.

The things sent to hurt us are the very things used to empower us. The things sent to destroy us are often the things that show us the Light of Christ. In all the sifting Satan desires to do to us, he has underestimated the God who desires the same thing. In the sifter, the crumbs are removed from the grease. The lumps are removed from the flour. The grains are removed from the coffee, to give it a smooth taste. So what, if the enemy has your crumbs! You don't need them anymore. They only hinder you. So, he has taken your lumps. Don't you realize he just made you more valuable?

Growing up, people would look at loose girls, girls like me, and say we had no value and no one would ever want to marry us. In the world, that may be so. However, we serve the God of the underdogs. He loves to take broken things and make them valuable. He loves to make a beautiful mountain out of a crushed molehill. Our pains and mistakes only add to our value when they are turned over to the hands of God.

In the aftermath of my pain and struggles with self, I can clearly see that every battle I had to fight was for my own good. I can now understand how the pieces of the puzzle of my past fit together to make me into a beautiful masterpiece, like a tapestry with light and dark threads throughout, displaying the grand craftsmanship of God.

For a very long time, I thought that no one could possibly ever understand or love me. I felt alone, abandoned, unloved and unwanted. None of those things were true, but those feelings ended up working for my good, hence, I now believe they served a necessary purpose in my life. Because of my perceived neglect, I withdrew myself from people. The loneliness made me grow more desperate every day. The desperation grew until it consumed me. No matter how many men professed an undying love for me, it was never enough. If I had one man or five, it was never enough. I still felt love-starved.

By the time God made His grand appearance in my life and proved His existence and love to me, I was so desperate for love that I found myself clinging to Him for dear life. My perceived lack of love made His love so much sweeter. It made it so much more real in my life. It made me appreciate God's love, though I didn't always understand His plan. The desperation that had always existed before never had a goal or target. After God came into my life, finally my desperation was aimed at something – getting closer to Him.

(I would like to insert a note here. There are people in churches that would tell you that what I'm saying is foolishness. There are people in the world that will agree. I'm not talking to those people. I am talking to people like myself... those who are tired of being in pain and turmoil. You've already tried everything else. What do you have to lose if you believe me and do it God's way? There is nothing that compares to His great love and His abundant mercy. There is nothing sweeter, no one kinder and gentler than our Heavenly Father.)

Sometimes, it hurts to love God so much. I have myself had times when I felt like I would burst wide open because my body couldn't contain what I

130

felt, my words were insufficient to describe it and God felt too far away for me to express it the way I desired. Still, in it all, I learned the meaning of my struggles. I learned that they were for Him, for me and for others.

In the aftermath, the attacks of the enemy didn't stop. In fact, Satan seemed to wage an all-out war against me. Sometimes, even knowing the greatness of God, I felt like I wanted to turn around and run away from Him. His ways felt too strict for me. I felt that I would never be able to please Him and sometimes, I got tired of trying. When I wasn't wrestling with flesh, I seemed to be wrestling with the devil. When I wasn't wrestling with him, it seemed that I was wrestling with God. Sometimes, I was wrestling with all three. More than a few times, I felt the truth of the old adage, "between a rock and a hard place."

It sometimes seemed the battles would never end. I can now stand and honestly say the way was not always easy. More times than I would like to admit, I *did* return to my old life and tried to resurrect the dead me and dead things. It would take many books to tell about all my shortcomings and failures, and many more to tell of my outright rebellion at times. I refuse to paint a rose-colored picture. The truth is what makes us free.

Nevertheless, God brought me through all my "times" and continues to do so. Let no one tell you that the aftermath of a battle doesn't come with trials of its own. It does. Let no one tell you that you won't experience more than one valley. You will experience many. Throughout your Christian life and walk, you will have many ups and downs. You will have many victories and some failures. You will have some setbacks and some delays. Still, it all works for your good because you love God and are the called according to His purpose. Every setback will show you a better way to accomplish your purpose. Every delay will work to increase your patience, which all men need in order to receive the promise. Every failure will teach you how to love God without His hand being involved. (You can only truly say you love God when you show it in droughts. Most people say they love Him, but what they really love is His hand!) Every down will prepare you to handle the ups.

God has divinely orchestrated the symphony of your life. Not one thing can take Him by surprise. He knows it all and knew it before you were even created. He has a loophole for every attack of the enemy which cause loses in your life. I was once told to stop playing captain of this ship called my life and things would get easier. I now pass that advice along: If you let go of your own autonomy, your walk with Christ, even in the tough times, will be much easier and much more peaceful.

There is no peace like the peace of knowing that God is in control. All you have to do is stand, having your loins gird about with truth. Be determined to remain strong. You are a soldier, and some of you are generals. Don't faint at the first sign of trouble. Stand boldly in your position of authority in Christ Jesus.

Ask yourselves, "With all that I've seen and been through, what is this in comparison?" It's only the aftermath. Tell yourselves, "I survived the hurricane. What is a spin off tornado or two?"

~Chapter 23~
Learn from Uriah

I certainly understand how easy it can be to get weary. I also understand how necessary it is to stay alert and be vigilant.

There is one unsung hero in the Bible. He is always portrayed as the victim of a selfish king. I want to go on record as saying that this alone is not all there was to Uriah, the Hittite. Uriah was a valiant man and a role model for us to look to in times like these.

There is a saying in the earth about saving the best for last. In the list of David's thirty mighty men in 1 Chronicles 11:25-47, toward the end is Uriah, the Hittite. In 2 Samuel, chapter eleven, we see Uriah refusing David's kindnesses. He refuses to enjoy himself while others are at war and possibly dying. He refuses to be intimate with his wife while others desire the same pleasure with their wives, but are not afforded it because of the war. Even in his intoxicated state, he doesn't lose sight of what is most important. He doesn't forget who he is.

One of the tactics of the enemy is to wear us down. He knows that when we are tired, we don't make the best decisions. We tend to try to find the easiest way out. No matter how strong, every person gets weak and tired sometimes. Even Uriah got tired and weary sometimes. He wouldn't be human if he didn't. The thing that separates him from many of us is that he refused to give in to the weariness. He refused to put himself first. He kept his goal ever before him. Because his priorities were set in order, he was able to push past his tiredness. He realized who he was in God- and to God.

We are no different than Uriah. We all have duties. We have a responsibility in Christ. We must not faint. Fainting is not an option. Once we realize that we don't have that luxury of stopping or resting on our own, we find that we can do a lot more and go a lot further than we had originally thought.

God knows when our limits are off yet a distance and when we truly need help. Regardless of what place we find ourselves in, we must learn from Uriah's character. We must be diligent, determined and steadfast. We can't afford to sit still too long. We must be ready to fight. Our minds must be girded. Our loins must be girded. We must always be ready for whatever may come next.

When we get off focus, this walk can seem daunting and downright tiresome. What makes a warrior a true warrior is not how well he or she can fight - it is their willingness to fight and even to die for what they believe. It is the determination to stay in the fight for as long as the fight may last. Real warriors are known for their tireless zeal and the continual preparations they make for the next battle. Warriors train themselves to love through or in spite of the battle without that love controlling their ability to function.

A movie called *300* came out this year. The battle scenes and the determination of the 300 warriors were staggering. To see them boldly stand up to millions of soldiers against all kinds of wiles and tricks, and yet prevail, was an eye-opening experience. Those 300 who were willing to die for freedom showed the millions that numbers count for nothing. It does not matter how many times the enemy attacks or how many different ways he attacks. What *does* matter is that you stand boldly knowing in whom you trust. We must be like the 300, though we may feel outnumbered and outgunned, there are truly more for us than those who are against us, so long as we stay the course that God has determined for us.

I remember preaching a sermon about storms and battles. They will never cease to exist, especially when you are doing the will of the Lord. The closer you come to fulfilling your destiny, the hotter the fire seems to become. The more you die to yourself and allow Christ to live through you, the more the enemy tries to deter you by any means necessary. Satan does not rest. He does not stop trying. He could be awarded a medal for his unstinting determination to hurt God by hurting us, God's most prized possessions.

Truly, we could learn a lot from the devil. We could learn never to be deterred from our purpose. We could learn the power of persistence. We could learn determination.

The same determination that we begin this walk in must carry us through all the storms, trials and troubles. The same confidence we had in God when we gave Him our sins is the same confidence we must keep throughout the days when God seems far away. The same zeal that consumed us when we were first introduced to Christ must be the same zeal that compels us to go through whatever we must in order to become who God says we are.

135

Chapter 24

The Beautiful Tradeoff

For everything the devil strips from us, there is something more wonderful, more necessary and more beautiful that God gives to us.

It took a lot of tears and pain for me to call my past a beautiful tradeoff. Indeed, it was so full of shame that only this book could make me face it all. It was so full of mistakes and missteps that only God could get me back on track. My past was so damaging that only God could repair me from it. For a long time, it consumed me, but God, through having me write this book, helped me to release the things that held me captive.

You, too, must go back and face the hurts of your past. You must face the memories and come to the place wherein you can release them. I have heard so many preachers say that we have all done things that we will never tell anybody. To that I say this: hiding things is a sign that deliverance has not yet come. When God brings deliverance from the pain and embarrassment of your past, you can and will tell it all to someone, anyone, for the benefit of the Kingdom.

Everything in your past belongs to God. He can use it when He desires to use it. Every mistake you made and every horrific thing that happened to you belongs to God. Once God helps you to deal with the past, it won't be hard to release all of your testimony. You will feel liberated enough to know that the person you speak of is dead. The hard things that happened to you helped make it possible for you to be birthed in Christ so that the person to whom those things happened can die.

In it all, there are three questions each person has to ask themselves. Who is it that lives through me today? Am I still fighting for my life? Does Christ truly live through me?

The answers are important. In order for us to give something to God, it must first be ours. You can't give away something that doesn't belong to you. That is a simple concept that is both natural and spiritual. We must first admit who we are and where we have been. Once we own or own up to those things, we can give them to God. When we release *us* to God, He hides our lives inside Himself. He leaves the memories and the body, but the essence of who we are becomes like Him. That is, in a nutshell, the beautiful tradeoff. God gets the rights to all of us: our memories, our flaws, our failures, our pain and our inner turmoil. We, in turn, receive His love, His acceptance, His forgiveness, His comfort and His covering. We get a rest that no one and nothing else can supply. We don't have to carry that burden of control and responsibility anymore. We become God's property. It becomes God's responsibility to lead and guide us. It becomes His responsibility to take care of us. He has control and our whole duty is to obey Him.

~Chapter 25~
A Word to the Hurting

If you are in pain over your past mistakes or over someone else's past mistakes that affected you, understand that there can be no glory from your pain until you release it to God.

I know what it is like to wait to be alone so you can cry your eyes out. I know what it is to feel alone though there are 20 people around you. I understand how hard it is to forgive someone whose actions seem to have ruined your life and destroyed your dreams. I understand the torment that comes at bedtime to tell you that your situation is your fault. I have felt the torment that seems to sing of your faults, failures and mistakes. You are not alone. These same things have happened before and will happen again to someone else. Herein lies the reason you are going through it. You must survive this now to help someone else through it in the future. Not everyone can endure what you are enduring. God might not allow people to be your comfort, but that's only so you can teach others how to lean solely on Him.

You must come to realize that most trials are designed to pull, to tug, to tear and to strip you. They are designed to stretch and push and cut at you. They are designed to make you run to God. They are there to teach you that God is our only answer. God knows you can come through it. You must not faint while the billows rise and the waves crash all around you. Stop calling to everyone else for the help that comes only from God. I'm not saying God won't use others to usher you through some things. In fact, there are times when He will. Even then, God is the source and not the people.

There may be times when you feel as if you have reached your limits; that place wherein your heart is so broken that there isn't any ministry, any hope, any peace, any joy, or any light left in you. You may feel that your self-image is so shattered that you would do more harm than good to keep living; there may be times when your eyes are so flooded with tears that you can't see straight. Your mind may seem stuck in the mire of self-doubt and self-condemnation. Yet, in this place comes the biggest blessing of them all. In this place, desperation consumes you. And if you will allow yourself to accept God and all His love and mercy, in this place, then that desperation will lead you into the greatest love anyone has ever known. In your desperate place, God can come in and show His glory and the abundance of His love on your behalf.

There are some people who cannot fathom how a "god" that is supposed to love us so much can allow such awful things to happen. For a long season, the humanity in me struggled with that same thought. I didn't understand how God could say that He, in His sovereignty, allowed my father to abandon me, so many men to have their way with me and my mother to never be available to me because of drugs. It took the pain and torment of Jesus Christ on the Cross to make me see that our lives are much bigger than we are.

Without a doubt, some of you are going to have a problem with this paragraph. I'm not trying to be controversial, but obedient. Some of us confess God's sovereignty with our mouths, but refuse to accept the fullness of that truth in our hearts. We want all the good things to be ordained and orchestrated by God. But, as soon as something bad happens, it was the fault of the devil. We cannot have it both ways. Though God is not capable of evil, nor does He tempt us with evil, He knew the end from the beginning. He took the movie of our lives, if you will, and made it backwards. He knows the shortfalls, where they will come from and how to save us out of them and utilize them later for His glory. Every hair on each of our heads is numbered by God. This is what sovereign means!

Without the pain Jesus experienced, there would be no salvation and remission of sins for us. God said it pleased Him to put Christ through those pains. It pleased God to see me come through those things I despised for so long. I've come to no longer despise my past, for the most part, but rather now I *mostly* appreciate the power God has given me to help others come through it. There was purpose in my pain.

Your pain has purpose. Every tear you shed pushes you closer to your destiny. It might not always feel worth all the drama, but once God dries your tears and lifts your head, it will seem a small price to pay for what will be eternally yours. Don't allow the lies the enemy yells at you to turn you despondent. Choose to focus on the whisper from God.

Allow God to whisper words of peace and hope to your spirit. Don't listen to those overwhelming feelings of despair. The enemy is relentless when it comes to making you feel that nothing is going right in your life. He will always try to bring depression upon you until you stand up and begin to listen to God and not your feelings.

I have included two of my writings from my journal and online blog. It was on my heart to include them in this book. The same God that healed my broken heart and wounded spirit is the same God that will do it for you. God bless you as you begin your journey into the desperation that will foster true intimacy with our Father.

Pages from my diary...

Fear of Abandonment
October 12, 2006

My testimony has been something often alluded to, but never really detailed for the public to know. I've guarded it like a close-held secret, refusing to let most people in. All the while, the Holy Spirit continues to deal with me to share it. I've been told that you can't share your testimony with just anybody. I've seen incidences in which I've shared my testimony with friends and indeed they used those incidences to judge me. Being the person I was, I'd learned to shut down. I can talk all day long and say nothing really meaningful... and this is the state of the world today- everyone's talking but saying nothing meaningful!

As people, and sometimes especially those of us of the household of faith, we have come to the conclusion that pain means something is wrong. When we open up to someone and they turn away from us, the pain of rejection causes us to close ourselves off. We have learned a most deceptive lesson: No man cares for our soul (for our mind, for our will, for our emotions). A scripture often misused for the purpose of closing the doors of our hearts. We should stop sharing ourselves.

As a child, I grew up feeling left out and otherworldly. I was never good at fitting in. I had plenty of friends, but on the inside, I never felt as if I truly belonged with anyone or anywhere. I was a loner by nature so that I never let my guards down.

*Being molested from before the time I was old enough to remember was a detrimental part of my childhood and adult make-up. Regardless of what experts say, the part of us on the inside that is pure God can tell when there is something wrong. We know it from a young age and we grow up with this "something" inside of us that just knows what we cannot explain. I knew at the ages of 4, 5, 6, 7, and 8 that being touched was wrong. I knew it in my heart and because I **was** touched it made me feel wrong. I felt abandoned.*

All that leads me to now...

When I am alone and all is quiet in my life, I can still hear God telling me that I'm not wrong, but I am precious in His sight. I am His creation, fearfully and wonderfully made. In my testimony to the world, I cannot give it accurately without the mention of my childhood. But the biggest part of my testimony comes not from what happened to me; rather it comes from what kind of person I became before God began to work on me.

I had low self-esteem because it seemed no one cared for me. I felt that I had no one. Because of my low self-worth in my own mind, I became a person with twisted morals and values. I would be with a married man, but not with my friend's man. I would steal from a store, but not from my family. I would fight my friends, yet still be willing to die for them. I wanted someone in my life, but had no clue how to allow anyone close to me. I wanted people to show genuine concern for me, but I didn't believe it when they did. I would end a perfectly good relationship, friendship or otherwise, because I thought it would hurt less if I did it rather than allowing them to walk away from me.

I found out this morning that my trigger in my flesh is fear of abandonment. The thing that opens old wounds and creates new ones is someone walking away from me. I used to call it separation anxiety. As hard as it is for me to admit, like many other women, I've allowed things to happen to me and kept quiet because I would rather take the wrong than be left alone. I thank God for a person who came through my life recently. He asked me a question that made me think even up to this day... he asked, "So, a person can cheat on you as long as he doesn't leave you?" My first response was no because no one wants to think of themselves like that. Desperate! Pitiful! Foolish! But, the resounding answer in my heart was yes and I knew it.

My prayer this morning is that God would heal those of us who fear being abandoned. For some of us, like me, it's not the aloneness so much as it is the loss of someone who seemed to care. Some of us have long ago separated ourselves because we cannot stand to lose another person that we love. Some of us are jumping from bed to bed to make ourselves feel like someone does care. Some of us are clinging to bad relationships just so we can believe someone cares. There is good news this morning... God cares. Bless His name... He truly cares!

I'm learning each day that even when I stand alone, I'm not alone. I can hear Jesus in the garden of Gethsemane talking to God. The 3 that He expected to stand with Him, at least in prayer, all slept while He agonized over what was to befall Him. Today, many of us are having that garden experience. We are agonizing alone. No one else seems to care enough to hold up our hands during our weak moments. They want to preach to us. They want to advise us. They want us to suck it up, but not one of them is willing to get in the trenches with us and quietly pray. Do you remember Job's friends? They exacerbated the situation with advice, when all that was needed was prayer and the support of their just being there.

One last thought on this subject: God never intended for us as His children to be alone. He said that it's not good that man should be alone. Babies need hugs and kisses and so do adults. Everyone needs love, and not in word alone, but in deed. God was alive and well when He said that man should not be alone. He knew, in His infinite wisdom, that as people of flesh, we sometimes need other flesh with us. So, before you begin to give or receive the bad advice about people needing to be alone, remember what our Creator had to say about it. Even when it's not time for us to be in a relationship with the opposite sex, God always intends for other saints to be there with us, encouraging us and pulling us higher. When He wants personal time, He knows how to pull us away to Himself.

Fear of abandonment comes because someone at some point in time walked away when we needed them most. Someone we trusted, someone that should have been there wasn't there. Our answer: God was always there. He will NEVER leave us. No matter how much bad doctrine and how many bad circumstances we come across, He understands us because He made us. He will comfort us when no one else is willing to. He loves us when no one else does. He will NEVER forsake the workmanship of His own hands... He will NEVER abandon us! Even when our mothers and fathers put us down, the Lord God will lift us up. He, though He can have whatever He wants, chose the dejected, deteriorated and weak things of the world for His own. Let us find rest in that when we can't find it in anything else!

Overflowing Love
January 09, 2007

I sit here tonight at the point of tears because of a love that is too big for my heart to hold, a consuming, burning, passionate love for my Father. I love God with my whole heart, and so often, it hurts to want to be so close to Him, but be limited by flesh. I understand when Paul says the whole creation groans awaiting the manifestation of the sons of God. We all have something in us that desperately desires our Lord.

We should love the Lord, our God, with all of our heart, all of our mind, all of our emotions, all we desire, all we can imagine or think, and with all of our might! It's okay to get caught up in emotions when loving on your Father. He gave them to you for a reason. It's okay to love Him mentally, physically and willfully. He wants our love in every way we can give it to Him.

For me, I passionately desire to be closer to Him. I wish a million times over that I could cry at His feet, or lie in His lap, or touch His cheeks. Nevertheless, my praise has to caress His cheeks like my hands would. My prayers have to fall upon Him like my tears would. Hallelujah! His love is extravagant, precious, priceless, wonderful, fulfilling, and full of splendor and majesty. He is faithful, true, merciful, forgiving, gracious, marvelous, loving and understanding. There's no bad in Him. Even His judgments are pure and righteous, marvelous in my eyes.

My words fail me tonight. Inside, there are a million words floating around my mind to describe the greatest love I've ever experienced. I feel as if I might spontaneously combust with the passion, love and desire in my heart for my Savior. He is my Dad. He has never and will never abandon me. For that, Lord, I tell you thank you. I am eternally grateful.

146

How has this book affected you? Even if you hadn't experienced the rape, incest, molestation or domestic violence, what have you experienced?

It's your turn to express yourself. Please use these journaling lines to express your feelings about this book or your life in general. Be sure to date each journal you write. A year from now, you'll be amazed at how far you've come!

Date: _____

Date: _____

Date: _____

Date: _____

Date: _____

Date: _____

_____
_____
_____
_____
_____
_____
_____
_____
_____
_____
_____
_____
_____
_____
_____
_____
_____
_____
_____
_____
_____
_____
_____
_____
_____
_____
_____

Date: _____

Date: _____

Date: _____

Date: _____

_____
_____
_____
_____
_____
_____
_____
_____
_____
_____
_____
_____
_____
_____
_____
_____
_____
_____
_____
_____
_____
_____
_____
_____
_____
_____
_____
_____
_____

RESOURCES FOR VICTIMS

If you've been victimized or know someone who has, please use these resources. Don't forget to find a church family. Never underestimate the power of prayer to heal and minister to your hurts.

Rape, Abuse and Incest National Network – the nation's largest anti-sexual assault organization; RAINN operates the National Sexual Assault Hotline and carries out programs to prevent sexual assault, help victims and ensure that rapists are brought to justice. For more information visit them online at www.rainn.org or for immediate, confidential help call the hotline at: **1-800-656-HOPE (1-800-656-4673)**.

Daily Strength – an online support community for victims of rape; you can speak with other people like yourself, get recommendations for medical professionals, and create confidential journals to share. For more information, please visit www.dailystrength.org.

National Domestic Violence Hotline – hotline for victims of domestic violence; promotes safety at home and in families; free, confidential and respectful. Call them now at **1-800-799-7233**.

OTHER RESOURCE NUMBERS

215-351-0010 ~ *National Clearinghouse for the Defense of Battered Women*

206-634-1903 ~ *Center for the Prevention of Sexual and Domestic Violence*

800-903-0111 ~ *Battered Women's Justice Project*

877-739-3895 ~ *National Sexual Violence Resource Center*